Richard Lovett

Norwegian pictures:

Drawn with pen and pencil: containing also a glance at Sweden and the Gotha Canal: with a map and one hundred and twenty-seven illustrations from sketches and photographs, engraved by E. Whymper, R. & E. Taylor, Pearson, and ot

Richard Lovett

Norwegian pictures:
Drawn with pen and pencil: containing also a glance at Sweden and the Gotha Canal: with a map and one hundred and twenty-seven illustrations from sketches and photographs, engraved by E. Whymper, R. & E. Taylor, Pearson, and ot

ISBN/EAN: 9783337724054

Printed in Europe, USA, Canada, Australia, Japan

Cover: Foto ©ninafisch / pixelio.de

More available books at **www.hansebooks.com**

Norwegian Pictures

Drawn with Pen and Pencil

CONTAINING ALSO A GLANCE AT

Sweden and the Gotha Canal

*WITH A MAP AND ONE HUNDRED AND TWENTY-SEVEN ILLUSTRATIONS
FROM SKETCHES AND PHOTOGRAPHS*

ENGRAVED BY E. WHYMPER, R. & E. TAYLOR, PEARSON, AND OTHERS

BY

RICHARD LOVETT, M.A.

LONDON
THE RELIGIOUS TRACT SOCIETY
56 PATERNOSTER ROW AND 164 PICCADILLY.
1885.

'The West Coast of Scotland is something like the nature of Norway in a general way, except that it is infinitely smaller and less grand; but that constant bright blue sky, those deeply-indented, sinuous, gleaming friths, those headstrong rivers and headlong falls, those steep hill-sides, those long ridges of fells, those peaks and needles rising sharp above them, those hanging glaciers and wreaths of everlasting snow, those towering endless pine-forests, relieved by slender stems of silver birch, those green spots in the midst of the forest, those winding dales and upland lakes; those various shapes of birds and beasts, the mighty crashing elk, the fleet reindeer, the fearless bear, the nimble lynx, the shy wolf; those eagles and swans and sea-birds, those many tones and notes of Nature's voice making distant music through the twilight summer night, those brilliant, flashing, northern lights when days grow short, those dazzling, blinding storms of autumn snow, that cheerful winter frost and cold, that joy of sledging over the smooth ice, when the sharp-shod horse careers at full speed with the light sledge, or rushes down the steep pitches over the crackling snow through the green spruce wood—all these form a Nature of their own. These particular features belong in their combination to no other land. And in the midst of all this natural scenery we find an honest manly race, not the race of the towns and cities, but of the dales and fells, free and unsubdued, holding its own in a country where there are neither lords nor ladies, but simple men and women.'

SIR G. W. DASENT: Introduction to *Popular Tales from the Norse*.

A BIT OF COAST NEAR MOLDE.
(*From a sketch by Professor T. G. Bonney*)

PREFACE.

THE object of this book is to give those who have not yet been able to visit Norway some conception of the wonderful beauty of the most accessible parts of that country. The volume may also serve to refresh the memories of those who have seen some of its fairest and most famous districts. Readers acquainted with the former numbers of the Pen and Pencil Series will readily understand that no attempt is here made to be serviceable to those who visit Norway to scale her highest peaks, to explore her most remote regions, to fish in her rivers and lakes, or to hunt the reindeer. The end aimed at has been to put before the general reader a series of word pictures and of engravings illustrating as fully as possible the broad features of Scandinavian scenery, from the North Cape to Christiania, and from Bergen to Stockholm.

The original plan was to call the book *Scandinavian Pictures*, and to include in it both Sweden and Denmark. This has not proved practicable within the limits to which every volume in the series is confined. Denmark has been omitted, and only the best-known and most beautiful parts of Sweden are described.

The author has visited all the most frequented parts of Norway and

Sweden, and no one can be more sensible than he of the impossibility of conveying, either by words or by engravings, any full or complete impression of such scenes as Trollhätta, the view from Krokleven or Stalheimsklev, or the midnight sun in the Lofoten Islands. He has however the strong conviction that in Norway, lovely and wonderful as the better known regions are, there must yet be in many parts waterfalls, lakes, and mountain views, quite as beautiful as anything known to the ordinary traveller. No effort has been made to discover and describe such scenes. His wish has been to produce a book that may afford to the reader something of the pleasure, stimulus and information that a journey through Norway's scenes of loveliness imparts.

The author has to acknowledge the kindness of Professor T. G. Bonney in placing one of his sketch-books at his disposal, from which some of the most interesting pictures in the book have been engraved, and also of Mr. G. H. Hodges, who placed at his disposal a series of photographs taken in the summer of 1884. Friends both in Norway and England have also helped in many ways. Most of the recent books on Scandinavia have been consulted. The author is indebted to the writers of these for much valuable information, and where they have proved of special service acknowledgment is made in the text.

A few hints on the pronunciation of Norwegian names will be found at the beginning of the index, and after each of the more unfamiliar names in the list an attempt is made to represent its sound.

CHILDHOOD.
(*From the painting by Tidemand in Oscar's Hall.*)

THE RETURN FROM THE WEDDING, HARDANGER FJORD.

VADSTENA CASTLE, GOTHA CANAL.

CONTENTS.

The Romsdal, near Horgheim . . . . *Frontispiece.*
A Bit of Coast near Molde . . . . *page* v
Childhood vi
The Return from the Wedding viii
Vadstena Castle, Gotha Canal ix

CHAPTER I.

THE KINGDOM OF NORWAY.

AREA AND POPULATION—CONFIGURATION OF THE COUNTRY—RIVERS, FJORDS, AND LAKES—CASCADES AND WATERFALLS—FAUNA AND FLORA—CLIMATE—RELIGION—CONSTITUTION—EDUCATION—TRAVELLING IN NORWAY. *pages* 13-26

Illustrations:

A Scandinavian Forest in Winter . . *page* 14   A Norwegian Church Porch . . . *page* 20
The Storthings-Hus (Parliament House), Christiania 15   Oscar II. 22
A Norwegian Pastor 18   The King's View, Krokleven, near Christiania . 25
       Kabelvaag, a Village in the Lofoten Islands 26

CONTENTS.

CHAPTER II.

SOME HISTORICAL PICTURES.

INFLUENCE OF THE NORSEMEN ON ENGLAND—NORWEGIAN LITERATURE—'THE GUEST'S WISDOM'—HAROLD FAIRHAIR—ROLF THE GANGER—HAROLD FAIRHAIR'S SON HAKON—THE ANCIENT AND MODERN YULE-TIDE—OLAF TRYGGVESON—OVERTHROWS HEATHENISM IN NORWAY—HIS SHIP-BUILDING—THE BATTLE OF SWOLD AND DEATH OF OLAF—HIS CHARACTER AND FAME—OLAF THE SAINT—AIDS ETHELRED TO REGAIN LONDON—GAINS THE THRONE OF NORWAY—HIS SHREWDNESS—CONVERSION OF DALE GUDBRAND—CNUT DRIVES HIM FROM NORWAY—DEFEAT AND DEATH AT THE BATTLE OF STIKLESTAD. *pages* 27-44

Illustrations :

The Viking's Ship . . . *page* 28	Celebrating Yule-tide . . . . . *page* 34
An Ancient Drinking-horn . . . 29	Hornelen, the cliff Olaf is said to have scaled . 38
Trondhjem Cathedral 44	

CHAPTER III.

FROM TRONDHJEM TO THE NORTH CAPE.

FIRST IMPRESSIONS OF TRONDHJEM—SUMMER EVENING LIGHT—HISTORY OF THE CATHEDRAL—SUNDAY MORNING SERVICE—THE CHOIR AND OCTAGON—ENVIRONS OF TRONDHJEM—MUNKHOLMEN—THE LERFOS—STEAMBOAT TRAVELLING—CHARACTER OF NORTH-WEST COAST OF NORWAY—MIST AND ITS EFFECTS—TORGHATTEN LEGENDS—THE LOFOTENS—HENNINGSVÆR—THE LOFOTEN FISHERIES—RELIGIOUS WORK AMONGST THE FISHERMEN—THE RAFT SUND—FIRST SIGHT OF THE MIDNIGHT SUN—A WONDERFUL LANDSCAPE—TROMSÖ—THE LAPPS—RELIGIOUS WORK AMONGST THEM—HAMMERFEST—THE SVÆRHOLT-KLUBBEN, OR GREAT BIRD ROCK—THE NORTH CAPE—THE MIDNIGHT SUN—VARDO—VADSÖ—THE LYNGEN FJORD. *pages* 45-84

Illustrations:

A Lofoten Village during the Fishing Season	*page* 46	Tromsö .	*page* 64
Trondhjem, the Ancient Capital of Norway .	47	Lapp Hut .	65
Thorwaldsen's Statue of the Saviour . .	50	Lapp Cradle . . .	65
Old Norse Boss, the Octagon, Trondhjem Cathedral	51	Herd of Reindeer in Lapland .	67
Old Norse Capital, the Screen, Trondhjem Cathedral	52	Lapps in Tromsödal . .	69
Old Norse Capital, the Octagon, Trondhjem Cathedral	52	Swedish Laplanders	70
		Sunday in Lapland .	74
West Front, Trondhjem Cathedral .	53	Hammerfest Harbour . . .	76
The Lesser Lerfos, near Trondhjem	54	The Sværholtklubben, or Bird Rock .	77
Torghatten from the East . . .	56	The North Cape	78
The Natural Tunnel through Torghatten	57	Part of a Group taken at Midnight, June 25, 1884	80
Henningsvær	58	Vardo	81
A Finland Fishing Boat . . .	60	Vadsö . . .	82
The Raft Sund	62	The Seven Sisters . . .	83
Hestmando		 84	

CHAPTER IV.

FROM CHRISTIANIA TO THE ROMSDAL.

CHRISTIANIA FJORD—CARL JOHANS GADE—THE VIKING'S SHIP—A STATE FUNERAL—SKETCH OF HANS NIEL HAUGE—AKERS HUS—OSCAR'S HALL—FROGNERSÆTER—LAKE MJÖSEN—THE GUDBRANDSDAL—THE ROMSDAL. *pages* 85-110

Illustrations:

Interior of an old Thelemarken House	*page* 86	Frognersæter	*page* 97
Christiania	87	Lake Mjösen and the Ruins of Hamar Cathedral	99
The Entrance to Christiania Fjord	88	View in the Romsdal, showing a Norwegian Road	103
The Akers Hus	94	The Slettafos	105
Oscar's Hall, Christiania	95	The Trolltinderne	106
Salmon Spearing by Night	96	The Romsdal Horn	107
The Stolkjærre			110

CHAPTER V.

THE WEST COAST AND FJORDS.

CHRISTIANSUND—MOLDE—MOLDOEN—HORNELEN—THE GEIRANGER FJORD—THE NORD FJORD—BERGEN—THE HARDANGER FJORD—ODDE—THE SKJÆGGEDALSFOS—ULVIK—EIDE—VOSSEVANGEN—THE NÆRÖDAL—THE SOGNE FJORD—LÆDALSÜREN—BORGUND CHURCH—OVER THE FILLEFJELD. *pages* 111-162

Illustrations:

The Nærödal	*page* 112	The Sand Vand	*page* 135
A Salmon Net and Stage	113	The Buarbræ Glacier	136
A Part of Christiansand Harbour	114	The Skjæggedalsfos	138
A Deck Passenger	115	The Tyssestrangene	140
The Boat coming off to the Steamer	116	The Spring Dance	141
A View in the Geiranger	117	The Vöringfos	142
The Seven Sisters Fall	118	View near Ulvik	143
The Horningdalsrokken	120	Glen near Eide	144
View from Faleide	122	The Sevlefos	147
Farm at Nedre Vasenden	123	Gudvangen and the Næro Fjord	149
Bergen	124	Borgund Church	152
Bergen Harbour	125	Bell Tower, Borgund Church	154
A Norwegian House of the Better Class	127	North Porch, Borgund Church	155
A Norwegian Peasant's House	128	Nystuen	156
A View on the Hardanger Fjord	130	A Snow Plough	157
Rosendal	132	Frydenlund	157
Hardanger Peasants	133	Hönefos	159
Odde	134	A Nook near Christiania	160

CHAPTER VI.

SOUTHERN NORWAY.

CHARACTER OF COUNTRY — THE KING'S VIEW—DRAMMEN — KONGSBERG — HITTERDAL CHURCH — THE RJUKANFOS — FLATDAL — A THELEMARKEN FARM — WOOD-CARVING — CHRISTIANSAND — SÆTERSDAL—STAVANGER. *pages* 161-176

Illustrations:

Gausta	*page* 162	Flatdal	*page* 169
The Old Chair in Hitterdal Church	. 163	Carved Lintel, Stabbur and Tankards .	. 172
Hitterdal Church . .	166	Part of Christiansand Harbour	173
The Rjukanfos	. 167	View near Stavanger . .	174
A Thelemarken Stabbur .		 176	

CHAPTER VII.

SOME HABITS AND CUSTOMS.

NORWEGIAN COURTESY—OWNERSHIP OF LAND—HOSPITABLE CHARACTER OF THE PRÆSANTRY—FARM-BUILDINGS—LIFE IN SÆTERS—MIDSUMMER EVE AND YULETIDE—PUBLIC WORSHIP—CONFIRMATION—' HOW ONE WENT OUT TO WOO '—WEDDING CUSTOMS—FUNERALS. *pages* 177-196

Illustrations:

Sunday in Norway . .	*page* 178	A Norwegian Bride wearing her Crown .	*page* 188
Girl Spinning in a Sæter .	. 179	A Norwegian Wedding . .	. 190
Interior of a Norwegian House .	182	Grandmother's Bridal Crown .	193
The Finishing Touch to the Toilet . .	184	The Wedding Procession .	195
Schoolmaster Catechising in Hitterdal Church	. 186	A Group of Dalecarlians	196

CHAPTER VIII.

FROM GOTHENBURG TO STOCKHOLM.

GOTHENBURG—THE GOTHENBURG SYSTEM—SMÖRGAS—ELSINORE—MALMÖ—SMAALAND—STOCKHOLM—UPSALA—LAKE MALAREN—THE GOTHA CANAL—MEM-BERG—MOTALA—WADSTENA—TROLLHÄTTA. *pages* 197-220

Illustrations:

A View in Smaaland .	*page* 198	The Castle at Upsala . .	. *page* 210
Gothenburg . .	. 199	Ancient Mounds at Gamla Upsala .	. 211
Elsinore . . .	201	Stegeborg Castle . .	. 212
Riddarholm Church, Stockholm	203	Toppö Falls, Trollhätta .	216
Stockholm . . .	206	The New locks at Akersvas	. 217
Upsala Cathedral .	208	Motala . . .	219
Linnæus . .	. 209	A View in North Sweden .	. 220

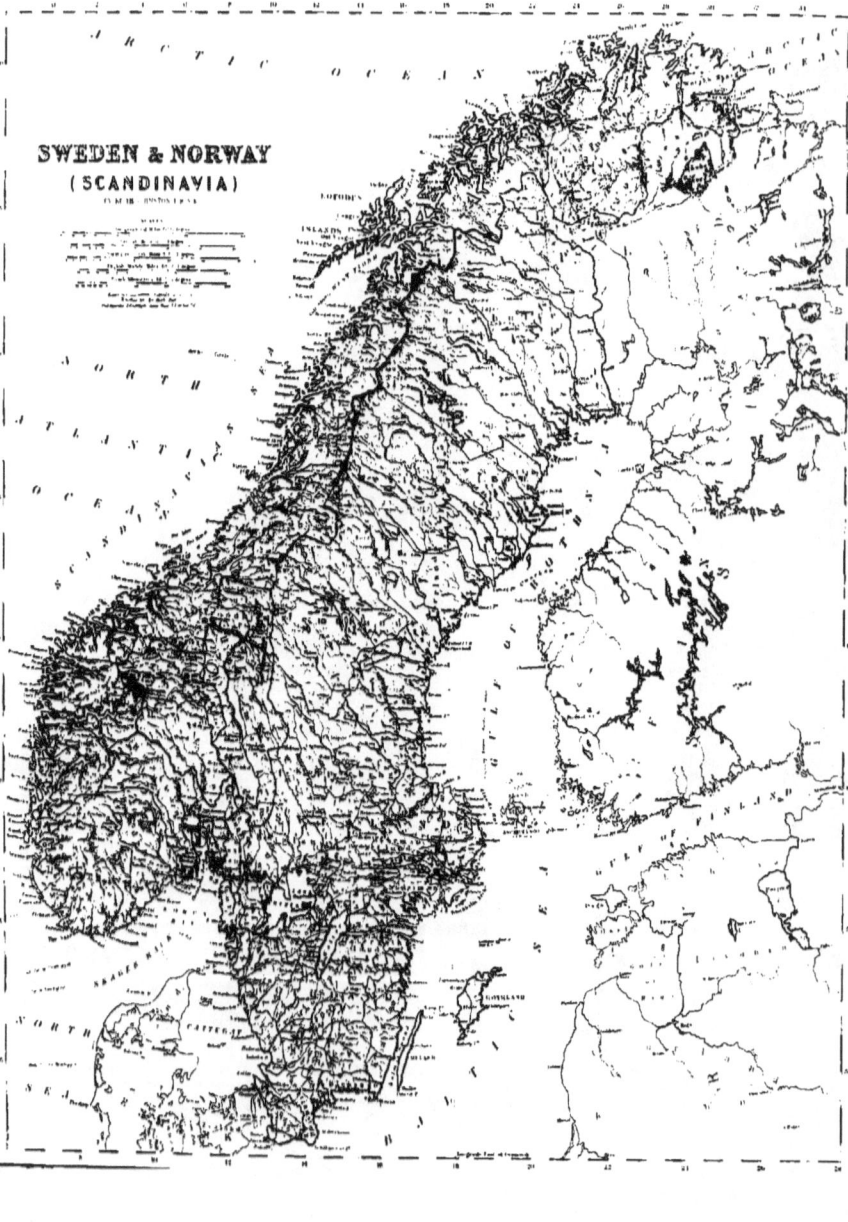

THE KINGDOM OF NORWAY.

A Scandinavian Forest in Winter.
(From a painting by Mindike.)

The Storthings-Hus (Parliament House), Christiania.

CHAPTER I.

The Kingdom of Norway.

Area and Population—Configuration of the Country—Rivers, Fjords, and Lakes—Cascades and Waterfalls—Fauna and Flora—Climate—Religion—Constitution—Education—Travelling in Norway.

THE kingdom of Norway occupies the western half of the great Scandinavian peninsula, the most northerly part of the continent of Europe. The length in a straight line from the North Cape to the Naze is 1030 miles, but the extent of the coast-line, *excluding* fjords, bays, and islands, is 3018 miles. The widest part is the belt of country which runs east and west a little north of Bergen, and is 280 miles across; the narrowest, the district near the Salten Fjord, about 70 miles broad. The area is 122,780 square miles, or a little more than twice as large as England. Norway is the most thinly inhabited country in Europe. The census for 1882 gave the total as 1,913,000, of whom 404,000 dwelt in towns, and 1,509,000 in the country. Of the chief towns, Christiania had 119,407, Bergen 43,026, and Trondhjem 22,152 inhabitants.

The country for about 300 miles south of the North Cape lies within the Arctic Circle, affording the visitor not only magnificent and unique scenery, but also the opportunity of seeing the "midnight sun," or, to speak more correctly, of seeing the sun go round the horizon without sinking beneath it.

At the latitude of the Arctic Circle this phenomenon can be seen for one day only; at the North Cape for nearly three months, from May 11th until August 1st.

The geology of Norway is too intricate a subject to be dealt with here, but it is needful to know something of the configuration of the country in order to understand the peculiarities of Norwegian scenery. The northern and western sections form a huge mountainous plateau, made up for the most part of gneiss rock, sloping gradually towards the south-east and abruptly towards the west. The western side has been cut into deep clefts and valleys. These great chasms in the plateau—due, in the opinion of some, to glacier action—form the far-famed valleys and fjords. The word *fjord* comes from the old Norse, survives in the modern words, 'firth' and 'frith,' is connected with the English 'fare,' meaning to travel, and used in the word 'farewell,' and meant most probably, in the first instance, water safe for navigation on account of its sheltered position. Hence it is also applied to lakes like the Randsfjord, and to arms of the sea like the Vestfjord.

North of Trondhjem, this mountain region forms a gigantic ridge, having its heights more peaked and regular, and its valleys deeper than the south country. The multitudinous islands also keep the pointed shape. Much of the distinctive beauty of the Nordland scenery is due to this peculiarity. South of Trondhjem the mountain region forms a plateau 2000 to 3000 feet high, with occasional peaks, such as Snehatten, 7566 feet, and Galdhöppiggen, 8400 feet. These mountain plateaus are called *fjelds*, from the old Norse word *fjeld* or *fjäld*, a corruption of the old Danish word *fjall*, meaning 'mountain,' surviving in our North-country word 'fell.' One result of the plateau shape of the Norwegian mountains is the formation of enormous snow-fields or glaciers, called *fonds*. Some of these, like the Folgefond, Jostedal Fond, and the Svartisen, cover from three hundred to five hundred square miles.

The rivers are for the most part streams which rush more or less rapidly down from the mountains and through the valleys into the fjords and lakes. The largest river in Norway is the Glommen, which, rising in the Trondhjem district, flows in a southerly direction, and at last empties into the Skager Rack at Frederickshald, forming, nine miles above its mouth, the fine falls of Sarpsborg.

Lakes are numerous in all parts of Norway, but they form a special feature of the scenery in the southern district of the country. The total area covered by them has been estimated at 2930 square miles. The largest are Lake Mjösen, 57 miles long, with an area of 200 square miles and a depth of 1483 feet, and the Randsfjord, 43 miles long.

The fjords occur at every part of the enormous coast-line, from the Varanger Fjord in the extreme north-east to the Christiania Fjord in the extreme south. They are of all sizes, and possess many individual peculiarities.

Sometimes they are sombre and wild, sometimes frowning and forbidding, and sometimes lovely beyond the power of words to describe, but never do they fail to charm those who sail on their placid waters. Among the chief are the Porsanger, a little to the east of the North Cape, eighty miles long; the Sogne and Hardanger, on the west coast, running inland for one hundred and eighty miles respectively; and the beautiful Christiania Fjord, forming, when traversed on a fine summer's day, the lovely approach to Norway's capital.

But not only is Norway the land of mountain and fjord; it is equally the land of cascades and waterfalls. These range from tiny silvery streams, adding loveliness to many a hillside, up to mighty masses of water that rush with thunderous uproar over cliffs 500 to 1000 feet high. The cataract and the *fos*, as the waterfall is called in Norway, are almost as common there as the hedge-row is in England. Many of the most famous, such as the Voring, the Skjæggedals, and the Seven Sisters, are pictured in this volume. But no illustration, no painting, can give more than a faint conception of their exquisite beauty, or convey even a distant approximation to the delight felt in watching the ever-changing yet ever-present forms of the falling water.

Norway possesses a considerable fauna, the chief members being the elk, the reindeer, the bear, the wolf, the glutton, the lynx, and the fox. The bears, though not uncommon, are not likely to attack human beings unless disturbed or wounded. The Government, however, pays twenty kronor (£1. 2s. 6d.) for every one killed. Although bears are occasionally seen, and nervous travellers are sometimes disquieted by rumours as to their nearness, most foreigners make Bruin's acquaintance only in the form of a somewhat tough, strong, but not altogether unsavoury dish at breakfast or supper at one or other of the large hotels.

Norway is rich in both sea-fowl and fresh-water birds. The golden eagle is sometimes seen. The magpie is abundant, and protected by the superstitious fear of the people, who will not kill it, although the Government offer three-halfpence a head for them. Crows also abound. There are also many game birds, the one most frequently met with being the *rippa* or *rype*, as they call it, better known in England as the ptarmigan. This is a tasty bird when placed before the hungry wayfarer for the first time, but he is apt to weary of it when he finds it garnishing every meal for a week or ten days.

Fish swarm in Norwegian waters, and the cod and herring fisheries, described later on in this volume, are of great value. Lobsters are caught in immense numbers, those found near Bergen having a great reputation. Salmon and trout abound—in fact, the traveller is in some danger of growing weary of both these toothsome fishes, inasmuch as they are rarely absent from his bill of fare. Most of the salmon-fishing is let to English and Americans.

The flora is rich in Alpine and Arctic plants, but, although flowers are to be found everywhere in the summer, it is not so rich as in countries farther south. The pine and the fir flourish, especially in the south. The birch is also very plentiful. The pine forests not only delight the traveller, whose road often passes through them, but also form one of the great staples of trade. In South Norway the cut logs are seen, covering large portions of the lakes, tumbling violently down the rapids and over the falls, and floating lazily down the rivers towards the sea.

The climate is on the whole very good, but the variations of temperature are very great, according to latitude, height, and distance from the sea. The sea tempers greatly the whole west coast, and thus, while Christiania Fjord freezes every winter, the main channels of the Sogne and of the Porsanger never do. The influence of the sea and the Gulf Stream is said to cause the average temperature of the west coast to be 36° higher than the corresponding latitude in other parts of Europe. On the coast the average temperature is 57°, on the fjelds about 50°. Around Christiania the thermometer rises to 86°; on the Finmark Fjeld in winter it sinks to 58° below zero. The rainfall near Bergen varies from 70 to 80 inches; near Christiania it is only 21 inches. There is no tide in the Baltic; but at Christiania it rises four inches, at Bergen about four feet, at Hammerfest nine feet. The people enjoy as a rule very good health.

A NORWEGIAN PASTOR.

In religion Norway belongs to the Lutheran Church. The country is divided into six dioceses or *stifts*, as they are called: Christiania, Hamar, Christiansand, Bergen, Trondhjem, and Tromsö. Each stift is presided over by a bishop, appointed by the Government. He is thus a State official, elected by a special committee of the Council, out of three candidates chosen by the vote of the clergy of the diocese. In the same way the Council chooses the incumbents out of three names selected by the parish. The result of this method of appointment has been to alienate to a great extent the active sympathies of the Norwegians from their Church. They are not

A NORWEGIAN CHURCH PORCH.

enthusiastically devoted to the King and Constitution, and they look upon the bishops and clergy mainly as part of the machinery of government. In the recent constitutional struggles the Church has sided with the King rather than with the Storthing. Probably on account of the tight hand kept over the Church by the State, men of ability keep aloof from it, and the great majority of the ministers come from the peasant-farmer class.

The dress of the officiating minister is strange to an English eye, consisting as it does of a long gown and a ruff like those common in England two hundred and fifty years ago.

The services at places like Trondhjem Cathedral or Vossevangen are for the most part well attended. The country churches also are fairly well filled. In many parts one service only is held, sometimes every other Sunday, sometimes once in three weeks. It is interesting to the stranger to see the peasants in their picturesque costumes, who very often have to travel five or eight miles to the place of worship. The churches are rude in design and finish, according to English ideas, but their quaintly-carved porches and pulpits and communion tables are always interesting. The most forcible impressions that a Norwegian service makes upon one not able to follow the language are that, although there is a good deal of singing, it is monotonous and unmusical to an English ear, and that the sermon, though generally animated, is not remarkable for brevity.

There are many Free Churches in different parts of Norway, belonging to the Baptist, Methodist, and other denominations. The pastors of these Churches are earnest, warm-hearted Christian men. They use hymns modelled after the Moody and Sankey type. They preach, simply and earnestly, the old Gospel, that 'the blood of Jesus Christ cleanseth us from all sin'; that 'God so loved the world that He gave His only begotten Son, that whosoever believeth in Him should not perish, but have everlasting life.' They believe in the Holy Ghost, and under His guidance and by His power they are doing much good and fruitful work.

These little assemblies have none of the formality common in the Established Lutheran Church, and they are gradually forming bands of active, energetic workers for Christ up and down the country. Many of the Lutheran clergy, especially those who magnify their office as servants of the State, resent the conduct of the Free Churches and their adherents. But upon many of the pastors it is having a nobler influence. It is stirring them up also to more energetic and faithful labour in the service of the one Master, the Lord Jesus Christ. In the Lutheran, as in all the Established Christian Churches, there are many faithful ambassadors for Christ, and these men, far from wishing to crush out the Free Church life, rejoice in its progress, and stretch out to it a helping hand.

A good deal of tract distribution is carried on in connection with the Lutherstift at Christiania, 499,700 being sent out in 1884; and every year, by the aid of the Religious Tract Society and other agencies, Christian literature is being largely circulated in Norway.

The Constitution of Norway dates from 1814, and under it Norway is a free kingdom, united with Sweden under one ruler. The form of government is a limited monarchy. Each kingdom is sovereign and independent,

Oscar II.

but in foreign relations they are considered as one, the ministry of Foreign Affairs being at Stockholm, and the foreign ambassadors received there. The King, who comes of age at eighteen, 'can do no wrong,' the responsibility resting upon an Executive Council, consisting of two ministers, and at least seven Councillors, among whom the State departments of Home, Finance, &c.,

are divided. Whenever the King leaves Norway, one of the ministers and two Councillors accompany him. The other minister acts as Prime Minister. The King appoints the ministers, who must be Norwegians by birth. It is in the King's power to declare war, to make peace, to conclude treaties, to command the army and navy, but Parliament must consent to offensive war, and it also controls taxation.

The Legislature of Norway is called the *Storthing*, or Great Parliament, and meets in a handsome building which forms one of the architectural features of Christiania. The number of members, by a law passed in 1878, is fixed at 114, the towns choosing thirty-eight, the country seventy-six. The members are not chosen directly by the voters, but they nominate electors, who in turn elect the members. Every Norwegian, twenty-five years of age, who, if resident in the country districts, is possessed of real property worth 300 kronor (£16), or who holds a public appointment, or who is resident in a town, and owns property worth 600 kronor (£33), has the franchise. Only those who possess the franchise, and are thirty years old, and have resided at least ten years in Norway, are eligible for membership. The elections are held every three years.

When the Storthing meets, usually at the beginning of February, a *Lagthing* or 'Upper House,' consisting of a quarter of the members, is appointed. The rest of the members form the *Odelsthing*, or 'Lower House.' All important measures originate in the Odelsthing. The Lagthing may pass, amend, or reject them. If passed, the royal assent makes the bill law. If rejected, the 'Lower House' again considers it. If passed again, it returns to the 'Upper House'; if it fails to pass, the whole Storthing meets, and a two-thirds vote carries it. The King has a veto, but a bill passed unchanged in three successive Parliaments becomes law.

The present King, Oscar II., has recently resisted this arrangement. After a long and somewhat angry struggle in 1884, he was constrained to yield, and even to allow the Storthing considerable power in such matters as the formation of the ministry and the control of the army. It is well known that King Oscar and the Queen are both earnest devoted Christians, who seek in all possible ways to use their high position and great opportunities to further the cause of the Gospel throughout their kingdom.

Norway ranks high among European countries in the matter of education. Even the sparsely populated districts are provided for by what is known as 'the ambulatory system,' that is, one master taking two or three parishes and visiting the schools in turn. In all parts of the kingdom many evidences of the attention paid to the instruction and training of the young are visible. At Hammerfest, far up within the Arctic Circle, there flourishes a good school with intelligent teachers and bright, happy-looking children. In 1878, 207,922 children were under instruction, in 6408 country schools, and 40,826 in 144 town schools. At the same time 15,800 were under training in the higher grade schools. The University of Christiania has a staff of fifty professors and an average attendance of one thousand students.

Norway differs from most Continental countries in having a very limited amount of railway. The only long line is that connecting Christiania and Trondhjem, a distance of 347 miles, the journey in summer occupying twenty-four hours. The character of the country is of a kind to make roads an expensive luxury.

The ordinary method of travel is by *carriole* or *stolkjærre*, curious little two-wheeled vehicles, the first carrying only one, the latter two travellers. These are drawn by wiry little Norwegian ponies. The roads, as a rule, are magnificent specimens of constructive skill, and are kept in order by constant care. Along all the main routes are posting houses under Government control, where horses are changed, where meals may be had, and accommodation for the night. The charges for the ponies and vehicles are fixed by Government.

Norway, if the writer may judge by the impression made upon himself, is unique among Continental countries in two respects. In the first place, it seems to possess a curious home atmosphere—that is, it does not appear to be a foreign land. True, the landscapes are unlike anything to be seen in England, the language is different, the sights and sounds are unfamiliar, and yet the wholly foreign feeling experienced when in France or Austria is wanting. In a way distinctly sensible, though difficult to describe, the English traveller feels himself to be in a kindred land. This impression may, of course, be purely subjective, or it may be due, in some subtle way, to the blood-relationship, which is much stronger than is generally supposed, between the two races.

And, in the second place, Norway is unique in the character and variety of its natural features. In the south the country is a network of lovely lakes, encircled by gently swelling hills, richly timbered, and abundant in flowers. In the west are found awful gorges like the Romsdal and the Nærodal, the Sogne and the Geiranger Fjords. The north exhibits the bold and conspicuous mountain scenery of the Lofoten Islands and the Arctic Circle, and in the interior the adventurous pedestrian finds peaks well worth climbing, and passes, snowfields and glaciers that can test endurance and delight the strong quite as fully as any Alpine region. Wherever the traveller turns his steps he finds natural beauties that refresh the mind, enchant the eye, and implant themselves for ever in the memory, ranging from scenes of savage and awesome sternness to views like that pictured on the opposite page, which, for its extent and beauty, is known as pre-eminently the King's View. The fact, too, that it is impossible to rush rapidly through the country lengthens out the enjoyment of the true lover of nature, and in some cases tends to create a love not before felt.

Those who cannot exist without all the luxuries of modern life had better avoid Scandinavia. Along many of the routes the wayfarer has to be content with such food as is placed before him, and such a couch as the small and sometimes crowded station can afford. Choice frequently there is none; but he will usually find the pure air a keen appetiser, and

THE KING'S VIEW, KROKLEVEN, NEAR CHRISTIANIA.

a day's ride in a carriole a good preparation for sound slumber, even though the bed be stuffed with straw, and shorter than a man can stretch himself upon.

He must be prepared to take people and things as he finds them, and if he travels with an open eye and a pure heart he will see much in the people to excite his interest and respect, and much in the country that will tend to emphasise the ancient Psalmist's words: 'The heavens declare the glory of God, and the firmament showeth His handy work.' Many a scene of unimagined beauty will give new force to the words of the modern Christian poet :—

> When heaven and earth were yet unmade,
>   When Time was yet unknown,
> Thou in Thy bliss and majesty
>   Didst live and love alone !
>
> How wonderful creation is !
>   The work that Thou didst bless !
> And, oh, what then must Thou be like,
>   Eternal loveliness !
>
> O Majesty most beautiful !
>   Most holy Trinity !
> On wings of faith we soar to get
>   A far-off sight of Thee !

KABELVAAG, A VILLAGE IN THE LOFOTEN ISLANDS.

SOME HISTORICAL PICTURES.

THE VIKING'S SHIP.

Showing: 1. The vessel when brought to Christiania; 2. As she must have looked sailing before the wind; 3. The rudder, oars, a shield and one of the tilt-heads.

AN ANCIENT DRINKING HORN.

CHAPTER II.

SOME HISTORICAL PICTURES.

INFLUENCE OF THE NORSEMEN ON ENGLAND—NORWEGIAN LITERATURE—'THE GUEST'S WISDOM'—HAROLD FAIRHAIR—ROLF THE GANGER—HAROLD FAIRHAIR'S SON HAKON—THE ANCIENT AND MODERN YULE-TIDE—OLAF TRYGGVESON—OVERTHROWS HEATHENISM IN NORWAY—HIS SHIP-BUILDING—THE BATTLE OF SWOLD AND DEATH OF OLAF—HIS CHARACTER AND FAME—OLAF THE SAINT—AIDS ETHELRED TO REGAIN LONDON—GAINS THE THRONE OF NORWAY—HIS SHREWDNESS—CONVERSION OF DALE GUDBRAND—CNUT DRIVES HIM FROM NORWAY—DEFEAT AND DEATH AT THE BATTLE OF STIKLESTAD.

THE influence of the Norsemen has been very great on the development of English life and character. Their annals furnish many striking heroes, and many thrilling and romantic incidents. There is also in English veins a very large admixture of the blood of the men who harried the monks of Holy Isle and Lindisfarne, who subdued Northumbria, who for a time ruled all England, and from whose stock sprang William the Conqueror.

The history of the lives and times of the men who made Norway what she was in the tenth and eleventh centuries, has suffered greatly from the legendary character and incidents imported by the later writers. The old Norse sea-kings and warriors, to whose influence much of the native strength and vigour of the English nature is due, are known to English readers mainly through Laing's somewhat bald translation of Snorri Sturleson's *Heimskringla*. But by the labours of modern scholars, notably Gudbrand Vigfusson of Oxford and his coadjutors, the real living men of the Viking age are gradually becoming known to us. To Vigfusson's Prolegomena to the *Sturlunga Saga* and to the *Corpus Poeticum Boreale*, edited by him and F. York Powell, the writer is greatly indebted, and in these books the latest and best information on this subject is found.

Whatever may be the true history of the origin of the Norwegian people, they manifested at a very early date a shrewd wit, a rough sense of humour, no great tendency to talkativeness, a strong love for the sea, and a delight in the fierce conflicts and savage deeds of war.

Thus in the earliest Norse poem known, entitled *The Guest's Wisdom*, a heathen production, wholly uninfluenced, as so much of the later literature is, by Christianity, such words as these are found:—

> No one can bear better baggage on his way than wisdom; no worse wallet can he carry on his way than ale-bibbing.
> He that never is silent talks much folly. A glib tongue, unless it be bridled, will often talk a man into trouble.
> One's home is the best, though it be but a cottage.
> No man is so good but there is a flaw in him, nor so bad as to be good for nothing.
> Middling wise should every man be, never over-wise. Those who know many things fairly lead the happiest life.
> Wakeful man's wealth is half won.
> Welcome becomes Wearisome if he sit too long at another's table.

It was not until the latter half of the ninth century—that is, a century or two after these terse proverbs were written—that the whole of Norway became subject to the rule of a king. Until that time the lordship was divided among a number of *jarls* or earls, who occupied themselves either in energetic efforts to destroy each other, or in the yet more congenial occupation of scouring the North Sea, and ravaging the coasts of Britain and Gaul.

At this time the shores of Christiania Fjord were known as the region of Vik, as it is usually spelt, but more correctly Wick. This word seems originally to have meant 'bay,' and to have designated what is now known as the Skager Rack, and the name Vikings—or, as it should be, Wickings— meant not 'men of the bays,' but 'men of *the* bay.' It was from this region that the earliest bands of sea rovers went forth to lay waste the coast of the North Sea. Ruling over the country at this date as far inland as Lake Mjösen, was an earl named Halfdan the Black, a strong, capable man, but chiefly notable as the father of a world-famed son.

At Halfdan's death, which happened about 860 A.D., his authority passed to his son, Harald Haarfagre, or, as he is better known to English readers, Harold Fairhair. In the later Sagas a story is told that early in life Harold fell in love with a beautiful girl, named Gyda, who sent his messenger back with this lofty reply: 'Tell to King Harold these my words—I will only agree to be his lawful wife upon the condition that he shall first, for my sake, subject to himself the whole of Norway.' This message enraged the royal messenger, but chimed in well with Harold's ambition. He at once vowed never to comb or clip his hair until he had either subdued the kingdom or died in the attempt.

He first conquered the Gudbrandsdal. He then extended his power over the Trondhjem region, and finally over the west coast, the deciding event being a great battle fought about 872, at Hafrs Fjord on the west coast, only a few miles from Stavanger. This great achievement occupied ten busy years, and at the end of that time he cut his locks and married Gyda. Harold's latter years were embittered by the quarrels of his numerous sons, and his efforts to satisfy their desires and arrange the succession. They lightened his task somewhat by killing each other to a very large extent, and his choice of a successor fell upon his favourite, Eric Blood-Axe.

Two incidents of special interest to Englishmen, and of great influence on English history, are connected with Harold's reign. An earl, Rognvald by name, a man of ability and conspicuous power, had been of great assistance to Harold in subduing Norway. He had a son named Rolf, called for some unknown reason the Ganger, a term commonly explained as meaning that he was too big for any horse to carry him, and was perforce compelled to become 'the Walker.' He was a proficient sea robber, and on one occasion, returning from an expedition and running short of provisions, he landed on the shores of Christiania Fjord, and, according to Viking custom, drove some cattle to the shore and slaughtered them for his crew. Harold had no objection to this in foreign parts, but allowed no oppression of his own people by his Vikings. A Thing or Parliament was assembled, Rolf was declared an outlaw, the entreaties of his relatives and friends were all in vain, and Rolf sailed off by way of the Hebrides, plundering to his heart's delight, and at last descended upon and made a permanent settlement in that part of Northern Gaul which has ever since been known as Normandy. The sixth in descent from Rolf the Ganger was a certain William the Conqueror, who was destined to exert a mighty and a permanent influence on English history. So that the 'cattle foray' on the shores of Christiania Fjord began, in a sense, the chain of events that resulted in the battle of Hastings.

The other incident, whether it actually occurred as given in the Sagas or not, gives us a picture of the men and customs of the times, and illustrates the intimate relations springing up between the rulers of Norway and England. During the closing years of Harold's reign, Athelstan was seated on the throne of England. One day ambassadors from Athelstan appeared at Harold's court and, displaying a magnificently jewelled sword, said: 'Here is a sword which King Athelstan sends thee with the request that thou wilt accept it.' Harold took the sword into his hand, and immediately the ambassadors said: 'Now thou hast taken the sword according to our King's desire, and therefore thou art his subject, as thou hast taken his sword.' This grim jest at first aroused Harold's anger, but, remembering that Athelstan was never likely to be able to derive any benefit from his sharp practice, the Norseman determined to pay him in his own coin. The ambassadors were well treated, and in due time dismissed. The next year Harold sent Hauk Haabrok, one of his favourite warriors, with a well-equipped ship to England, intrusting to his care his son Hakon. With thirty of his men Hauk entered Athelstan's hall in London at the time of a great feast. Saluting the king, he placed, greatly to Athelstan's surprise, the child Hakon upon his knee. In reply to the king's question, Hauk, probably with a merry twinkle in his eye, rejoined: 'Harold the King bids thee foster his child.' Athelstan seized a sword, and was about to slay the child, when Hauk rejoined: 'Thou hast borne him on thy knee, and thou canst murder him if thou wilt; but thou wilt not make an end of all King Harold's sons by so doing.' The point of the incident is that one who fosters another's child ranks lower than the father of the fostered child. Snorri, in his *Chronicle of the Kings of Norway*, hereupon says: 'From these transactions between the two kings it appears that each wanted to be held greater than the other; but in truth there was no injury to the dignity of either, for each was the upper king in his own kingdom until his dying day.'

Athelstan discharged well his duties towards Hakon, had him 'baptised, and brought up in the right faith and in good habits, and all sorts of exercises;' and the boy was worthy of his care, for he has come down to us as one beloved of all, and known as Hakon the Good.

Harold Fairhair died about 933 A.D., and Eric Blood-Axe, by reason of his cruelties, became so unpopular that Hakon was invited to leave England and take the kingdom. He came, and when he spoke to the assembled nobles, as they heard him they said: 'Harald Haarfagre is come again and grown young.' Eric sailed away to the Orkneys, and was for some time Earl of Northumbria, where he soon died.

Harold Fairhair's reply to Athelstan's jest led to important results. Hakon had been trained in the Christian faith, and as soon as he was firm in his seat at Norway 'he sought to introduce Christianity.' 'He went to work first by enticing to Christianity the men who were dearest to him; and many out of friendship to him allowed themselves to be baptised, and some laid aside sacrifices.' But all customs are not easily rooted out, and the sacrifices died hard. At Yuletide there were great sacrifices and feastings, and there were scenes oftentimes of wild revelry and excess, and generally the king took a prominent part. Hakon's manifest desire to abolish these heathen feasts met with little favour, and his nobles at last told him that in the matter of religion they must have their own way. On one occasion the bonders or peasants insisted on the king's presence, and Earl Sigurd of Trondhjem, taking the first goblet, blessed it in Woden's name and drank to the king. Hakon then took the horn, made the sign of the cross over it, and drank. But his movement had been seen; and, in reply to angry demands as to its meaning, the ready Sigurd replied: 'He is blessing the full goblet in the name of Thor by making the sign of his hammer over it before he drinks.'

King Hakon died without seeing his cherished wish fulfilled, but it is pleasant to look back through the centuries and dimly discern the figure of the man who first eagerly desired to win his brave, vigorous countrymen for Christ.

The old heathen gods and beliefs, with their savage and repulsive ceremonies and orgies, passed away eight centuries ago. But the season of Yuletide or Christmas is observed as zealously as in King Hakon's day, only with much milder and happier customs. The feast begins on *Jul Aften*, or Christmas Eve. The whole household meet together, and with what store they have they feast. It is a time of rejoicing, of fun and frolic, of relaxation from the sterner duties of life, and forgetfulness, so far as may be, of its frets and cares. The children share in it, and dances, music, and games of all kinds enliven the days. The lower creation shares in the general joy, and even the birds are remembered, a sheaf of oats being fastened to the roof for their enjoyment. A representation is given in the engraving on the next page of what Christianity in Norway has put in the place of the old heathen Yuletide sacrifice and feast.

After a reign of twenty-six years Hakon was surprised by an army under the sons of Eric Blood-Axe, about 961. The battle fills a large space in the Sagas, and was won by Hakon's army, though at the cost of their leader's life. He left only a daughter, and desired that Eric's sons might succeed him. 'So great,' says Snorri, 'was the sorrow over Hakon's death that he was lamented both by friends and enemies, and they said that never again would Norway see such a king.'

The two great heroes of the Sagas are Olaf Tryggveson and Olaf the Saint. The former was a great-grandson of Harold Fairhair; and although the facts of his life are now fairly well known, there has been engrafted upon them a second life of fable and legend. It is to the latter that the commonly accepted story of his life belongs.

His early manhood was spent in the wild adventures and fierce fightings of the palmy days of the Vikings. He fought on English soil at Sandwich, Ipswich and Maldon. He aided Sweyn in his attempt to seize London, and, after harrying the southern counties and wintering at Southampton, they received £16,000 from the King of England as Danegelt. He came under Christian influence, and, although the ordinary accounts of his conversion are apocryphal, he certainly gave up his heathenism and made a promise, which he kept, never to invade England again. He also married, but who and where is uncertain. The later story describes how an Irish princess, seeing him in the dress of a man of low rank, was so impressed by his appearance that she chose him for her husband.

Meanwhile in Norway the usual internecine wars had been carried on bravely, and Hakon, son of Sigurd, Earl of Trondhjem, having obtained supreme power, held it for some years, but used it so badly in the end as to become

CELEBRATING YULE-TIDE.
(From a painting by A. Tidemand.)

very unpopular. Olaf's fame had spread, and Hakon is said to have sent a spy, Thorer by name, to ascertain the truth, and, if possible, arrange to have him put out of the way. Thorer informed Olaf of the state of affairs in Norway, and induced him to set sail thither. On landing Olaf found the country in rebellion against Hakon, who was slain by a slave named Karker, who brought Hakon's head to Olaf, and got swift execution for his pains. 'King Olaf,' runs the chronicle, 'and a vast number of bonders with him, then went out to Nidarholm [Munkholmen, in Trondhjem Bay], and had with them the heads of Earl Hakon and Karker. This holm was used then for a place of execution of thieves and ill-doers, and there stood a gallows on it. He had the heads of the earl and of Karker hung upon it, and the whole army of the bonders cast stones at them.'

Hakon was the last of the old heathen kings, and a touch of regret can be traced in the Saga: 'Earl Hakon was very generous; but the greatest misfortunes attended even such a chief at the end of his days; and the great cause of this was, that the time was come when the heathen sacrifices and idolatrous worship were doomed to fall, and the holy faith and good customs to come in their place.'

A General Thing chose Olaf king over the land, and he at once brought it all under his rule. As soon as he was fairly settled in his seat, he began to introduce Christianity. In Wick he invited every man to accept Christianity, and by his words and influence won over many of the people, strengthening his power by giving his two step-sisters in marriage to two of his nobles.

At one of the Things convened on the matter the king spoke at length, without, however, convincing his hearers; but the three bonders who had been appointed to conduct the case for heathenism broke down (according to Snorri): the first through a violent fit of coughing, the second from nervousness, and the third from finding himself too hoarse to be able to speak. Accordingly all present were baptised!

At Trondhjem his efforts to establish Christianity were stoutly opposed. A Thing was assembled, but the bonders rudely broke in upon the king's speech, and called out on him to be silent, or they would attack him and drive him away. 'We did so,' said they, 'with Hakon, foster-son of Athelstan, when he brought us the same message, and we held him in quite as much respect as we hold thee.' Olaf saw that caution was needful, and so he spoke gently to them, and said that he would himself appear at their Midsummer sacrifice. He came in due course with his men, and said that they had refused to be baptised at his request, and had invited him to the sacrifices. He had come, and meant to observe them in superior fashion. 'If I along with you shall turn again to making sacrifice, then will I make the greatest of sacrifices that are in use; and I will sacrifice men. But I will not select slaves or malefactors for this, but will take the greatest men only to be offered to the gods'; and he named eleven of the chief men present. As the king was too strong to be gainsaid, this settled the matter;

the nobles preferred baptism to immolation, and Christianity was established in the Trondhjem region. Be this story as it may, it was not without bloodshed that, in this instance, the change of creed took place, for a chief surnamed Ironbeard was slain.

Olaf was most devoted in the great missionary work, and there seems to be no doubt that many of the incidents told in the later Sagas of Olaf the Saint's efforts belong really to his history. It may have been a somewhat rough method, and the Christianity introduced was probably of a very inferior type; but teachers followed, and the power of Woden rapidly waned before that of the White Christ, and soon the human sacrifices, the savage feastings, and the wild carousals became things of the past.

Olaf's political capacity appears in his foundation of Nidaros, or, as it is now called, Trondhjem, for we read: 'King Olaf with his people went out to Nidaros, and made houses on the flat side of the river Nid, which he raised to be a merchant town, and gave people ground to build houses upon.' He probably aimed at founding a great Christian empire on the Baltic.

Later on Olaf made proposals for marriage with Sigrid the Haughty, a Swedish queen (here again the story becomes somewhat legendary), who, on one occasion, finding the attentions of two royal suitors troublesome, lodged them in the same house, set fire to it in the night, and consumed them both. 'As she stoutly refused to become a Christian, Olaf flew in a passion: "Why should I care to have thee, an old faded woman; and a heathen jade?" and therewith struck her in the face with his glove, which he held in his hand, rose up, and they parted. Sigrid said: "This may some day be thy death!" And so in the end it proved.'

Olaf devoted much time and attention to ship-building. The Crane was famous, but was soon eclipsed by the Short Serpent, which in turn, a year later, was surpassed by the still more noted Long Serpent. It was on board this masterpiece of the ship-builder's art that he fought his last battle. Sweyn Forked Beard, who afterwards conquered England, was ruling Denmark at this time. He married Sigrid the Haughty, whom Olaf had so grievously offended. On his way back from an expedition to Wendland, Olaf was waylaid by Sweyn and the Norwegian earls in alliance with him. A great battle was fought, of which a long description is given in the Saga. Earl Eric, Hakon's son, fought on Sweyn's side. 'Who owns the large ships on the larboard side of the Danes?' asks Olaf, as they draw near. 'That is Earl Eric, Hakon's son,' say his men. The king replies: 'He, methinks, has good reason for meeting us; and we may expect the sharpest conflict with these men, for they are Norsemen like ourselves.'

And so it came to pass. The Danes yielded, but the Norsemen stood their ground. In their frenzy many of Olaf's men forgot they were on ship-board, and fell into the sea and were drowned. Stripped of later addition, this probably means that they broke their shield wall by boarding the enemy's ships. Eric stood erect on his ship's deck, and Einar, Olaf's chief archer, tried to shoot him.

'Einar shot an arrow at Earl Eric, which hit the tiller end just above the earl's head so hard that it entered the wood up to the arrow-shaft. Then said the earl to a man called Fin: "Shoot that tall man by the mast." Fin shot, and the arrow hit the middle of Einar's bow, just at the moment that Einar was drawing it, and the bow was split in two parts. "What is that," cried King Olaf, "that broke with such a noise?" "Norway, king, from thy hands!" cried Einar. And so it proved, for, although the battle raged long and desperately, victory declared against Olaf. The Long Serpent was boarded, one by one her brave defenders were slain, and at last, seeing that all was lost, Olaf sprang overboard, shield on his arm, and sank beneath the waves. The battle was fought September 9th, 1000.'

Olaf had powerfully affected the popular affection and imagination of his day. His people refused to believe that he was dead. Wonderful ways of escape were described, but Olaf never again was seen by mortal man. The conquerors divided Norway among themselves.

Olaf Tryggveson still lives in the popular imagination of the Scandinavian people. Prints of his feats are to be seen in the humble cottage, paintings and sculptures in the museums and public institutions. In his romantic adventures, in his ready wit, in his dauntless bravery, in his splendour as a ship-builder, in his skill as a captain, and in his energy as a religious reformer, he became the typical Norse hero for after times. He ruled Norway only five years, from 995 to A.D. 1000, and perhaps the shortness and vigour of his rule helped to establish his fame. The chronicle says of him: 'King Olaf was more expert in all exercises than any man in Norway whose memory is preserved to us in the Sagas; and he was stronger and more agile than most men, and many stories are written down about it. One is that he ascended the Smalsor Horn (Hornelen), and fixed his shield upon the very peak. He could run across the oars outside of the vessel while his men were rowing the Serpent. He could play with three daggers, so that one was always in the air, and he took the one falling by the handle. He could walk all round upon the ship's rails, could strike and cut equally well with both hands, and could cast two spears at once. King Olaf was a very merry, frolicsome man, gay and social; had great taste in everything; was very generous, very careful in his dress, but in battles he exceeded all in bravery.'

'The greatest of all the northern kings,' write Vigfusson and Powell of Olaf Tryggveson, 'his life is an epic of exceeding interest. Coming out of the darkness, he reigns for five short years, during which he accomplishes his great design, the Christianising of Norway and all her colonies; and then, in the height of all his glory, with the halo of holiness and heroism undimmed on his head, he vanishes again. But his works do not perish with him. He had done his work, and though maybe his ideal of a great Christian empire of the Baltic was unfulfilled, he had, single-handed, wrought the deepest change that has ever affected Norway. His noble presence brightens the Sagas wherever it appears, like a ray of sunshine gleaming across the dark shadowy depths of a northern firth. All bear witness to the wonderful charm which his personality exercised over all that were near him, so that, like the holy King Lewis (who, however, falls short of Olaf), he was felt to be an unearthly superhuman being by those who knew him. His singular beauty, his lofty stature, golden hair, and peerless skill in bodily feats, make him the typical Norseman of the old heroic times—a model king.'[1]

The other great Norse hero is Olaf

[1] *Corpus Poeticum Boreale*, ii. 83.

HORNELEN, THE CLIFF OLAF IS SAID TO HAVE SCALED.
(*From a sketch by Professor T. G. Bonney.*)

Haroldsson, known to all later times as Olaf the Saint. His father, Harold Grænske, was one of the two suitors said to have been burnt by Sigrid the Haughty. Olaf entered upon the Viking life at the age of twelve, and thirteen of his battles are recorded in the Sagas. He happened to be in Normandy when Sweyn, king of England, died, and he supported Ethelred in an attempt to regain his crown. In Lent, 1014, his fleet carried Ethelred back to his native soil. An attack was made upon London, a description of which is here given as it stands in. Laing's translation of Olaf's Saga.

'On the other side of the river is a great trading place which is called Sudrviki (Southwark). There the Danes had raised a great work, dug large ditches, and within had built a bulwark of stone, timber, and turf, where they had stationed a strong army. King Ethelred ordered a great assault, but the Danes defended themselves bravely, and King Ethelred could make nothing of it. Between the castle and Southwark there was a bridge, so broad that two waggons could pass each other upon it. On the bridge were raised barricades, both towers and wooden parapets, in the direction of the river, which were nearly breast high; and under the bridge were piles driven into the bottom of the river. Now when the attack was made the troops stood on the bridge everywhere, and defended themselves. King Ethelred was very anxious to get possession of the bridge, and he called together all the chiefs to consult how they should get the bridge broken down. Then said King Olaf, he would attempt to lay his fleet alongside of it, if the other ships would do the same. It was then determined in this council that they should lay their war forces under the bridge; and each made himself ready with ships and men.

'King Olaf ordered great platforms of floating wood to be tied together with hazel bands, and for this he took down old houses; and with these as a roof he covered over his ships so widely that it reached over the ships' sides. Under this screen he set pillars so high and stout that there both was room for swinging their swords, and the roofs were strong enough to withstand the stones cast down upon them. Now when the fleet and men were ready, they rowed up along the river; but when they came near the bridge, there were cast down upon them so many stones and missile weapons, such as arrows and spears, that neither helmet nor shield could hold out against it; and the ships themselves were so greatly damaged that many retreated out of it. But King Olaf, and the Northmen's fleet with him, rowed quite up under the bridge, laid their cables around the piles which supported it, and then rowed off with all the ships as hard as they could down the stream. The piles were thus shaken in the bottom, and were loosened under the bridge. Now as the armed troops stood thick of men upon the bridge, and there were likewise many heaps of stones and other weapons upon it, and the piles under it being loosened and broken, the bridge gave way; and a great part of the men upon it fell into the river, and all the others fled, some into the castle, some into Southwark. Thereafter Southwark was stormed and taken. Now when the people in the castle saw that the river Thames was mastered, and they could not hinder the passage of ships up into the country, they became afraid, surrendered the tower, and took Ethelred to be their king. So says Ottar Swarte :—

> London bridge is broken down,
> Gold is won, and bright renown.
>   Shields resounding,
>   War horns sounding,
> Hildur shouting in the din!
>   Arrows singing,
>   Mail-coats ringing—
> Woden makes our Olaf win!'

Cnut, Sweyn's son, relinquished for a time his hold on London and the south of England, but only to return and accomplish a still more terrible and complete conquest than that achieved by Sweyn. Olaf meanwhile sailed off to Norway, which he found the more exposed to his power, as so many of the earls had hastened to the plunder of England under Cnut's leadership. On Palm Sunday, 1015, he defeated, in the Trondhjem district, Earl Sweyn, who had been left in charge of Norway, and obtained the supreme power.

The Sagas abound in stories that, even if they do not always enshrine facts, enable us to see what kind of qualities the man possessed about whom they cluster. The most striking facts brought to light by modern research appear to be those which tend to prove that Olaf Tryggveson was the real religious reformer and missionary king, and that Olaf, though handed down to posterity as the saint, was essentially a shrewd, practical secular ruler.

'He was no Olaf Tryggveson come back,' write Vigfusson and Powell, 'as the people hoped, this short, thick-set, ruddy young man, that carried his head slightly stooping, like the hard thinker he was. Here was a lover of order, who drove the courts, enforced the laws with the strong hand, and who, as other kings in like case, ruled through men he could trust rather than the nobles whom he suspected; who was the organiser of the public and the church law, and the severe scourge of those that broke it—such was Norway's saint that was to be.'

The following incident from the Sagas illustrates at once the wit and readiness of the king and his shrewdness in getting rid of uncomfortable and dangerous neighbours. The Rærek mentioned at the close was an old blind earl who more than once had attempted the king's life :—

'King Olaf had Thorarin with him as a guest for some days, and conversed much with him; and Thorarin even slept in the king's lodgings. One morning early the king awoke while the others were still sleeping. The sun had newly risen in the sky, and there was much light within. The king saw that Thorarin had stretched out one of his feet from under the bed-clothes, and he looked at the foot awhile.

'In the meantime the others in the lodging awoke; and the king said to Thorarin: "I have been awake for a while, and have seen a sight which was worth seeing; and that is a man's foot so ugly that I do not think an uglier can be found in this merchant town." Thereupon he told the others to look at it, and see if it was not so; and all agreed with the king. When Thorarin observed what they were talking about, he said: "There are few things for which you cannot find a match, and that may be the case here."

'The king says, "I would rather say that such another ugly foot cannot be found in the town, and I would lay any wager upon it."

'Then said Thorarin: "I am willing to bet that I shall find an uglier foot still in the town."

'The king: "Then he who wins shall have the right to get any demand from the other he chooses to make."

'"Be it so," said Thorarin. Thereupon he stretches out his other foot from under the bed-clothes, and it was in no way handsomer than the other, and moreover wanted the little toe. "There," said Thorarin, "see now, king, my other foot, which is so much uglier; and, besides, has no little toe. Now I have won."

'The king replies: "That other foot was so much uglier than this one by having five ugly toes upon it, and this has only four; and now I have won the choice of asking something from thee."

'"The sovereign's decision must be right," says Thorarin; "but what does the king require of me?"

'"To take Rærek," said the king, "to Greenland, and deliver him to Leif Ericsson."'

The following story occurs in Olaf's Saga, and illustrates the curious mixture of fact and fiction in the later Norse literature. It seems established now that the Norsemen had *no* idols, and there is much evidence to prove that the conversion of Gudbrand and his men took place in the life of Olaf Tryggveson. But that the conversion did take place is certain, and the story may be given as it stands in Laing's translation as an instance of the play that the later Norse writers gave to their imagination. The bonders of the uplands or north country district had met to consider the king's proposals. He was accompanied, among others, by a chief named Kolbein, who wielded a mighty club. The story runs:—

'The king told Kolbein to stand nearest to him in the morning, and gave orders to his people to go down in the night to where the ships of the bonders lay and bore holes in them, and to let loose their horses on the farms where they were: all which was done. Now the king was in prayer all the night, beseeching God of His goodness and mercy to release him from evil. When mass was ended, and morning was grey, the king went to the Thing. When he came there, some bonders had already arrived, and they saw a great crowd coming along, and bearing among them a huge man's image, glancing with gold and silver. When the bonders who were at the Thing saw it they started up, and bowed themselves down before the ugly idol. Thereupon it was set down upon the Thing-field; and on the one side of it sat the bonders, and on the other the king and his people.

'Then Dale Gudbrand stood up, and said, "Where now, king, is thy God? I think He will now carry His head lower: and neither thou, nor the man with the horn whom ye call bishop, and sits there beside thee, are so bold to-day as on the former days; for now our god, who rules over all, is come, and looks on you with an angry eye; and now I see well enough that ye are terrified, and scarcely dare to raise your eyes. Throw away now all your opposition, and believe in the god who has all your fate in his hands."

'The king now whispers to Kolbein Sterki, without the bonders perceiving it: "If it come so in the course of my speech that the bonders look another way than towards their idol, strike him as hard as thou canst with thy club."

'The king then stood up and spoke: "Much hast thou talked to us this morning, and greatly hast thou wondered that thou canst not see our God; but we expect that He will soon come to us. Thou wouldest frighten us with thy god, who is both blind and deaf, and can neither save himself nor others, and cannot even move about without being carried; but now I expect it will be but a short time before he meets his fate: for turn your eyes towards the east—behold our God advancing in great light."

'The sun was rising, and all turned to look. At that moment Kolbein gave their god a stroke, so that the idol burst asunder; and there ran out of it mice as big almost as cats, and reptiles, and adders. The bonders were so terrified that some fled to their ships, but when they sprang out upon them they filled with water, and could not get away. Others ran to their horses, but could not find them. The king then ordered the bonders to be called together, saying he wanted to speak to them, on which the bonders came back, and the Thing was again seated.

'The king rose up and said: "I do not understand what your noise and running mean. Ye see yourselves what your god can do—the idol ye adorned with gold and silver, and brought meat and provisions to. Ye see now that the protecting powers who used it were the mice and adders and reptiles; and they do ill who trust to such, and will not abandon this folly. Take now your gold and ornaments that are lying strewed about on the grass, and give them to your wives and daughters, but never hang them hereafter upon stock or stone. Here are now two conditions between us to choose upon: either accept Christianity, or fight this very day; and the victory be with them to whom the God we worship gives it."

'Then Dale Gudbrand stood up and said: "We have sustained great damage upon our god; but, since he will not help us, we will believe in the God thou believest in."

'Then all received Christianity. The bishop baptised Gudbrand and his son. King Olaf and Bishop Sigurd left behind them teachers, and they who met as enemies parted as friends; and Gudbrand built a church in the valley.'

Olaf reigned over Norway for ten years, but Cnut had not forgotten that assistance he had given to Ethelred. Having firmly seated himself upon the throne of England, he summoned Olaf to acknowledge his suzerainty. He refused, and Cnut invaded Norway. All those who disliked the strong hand of justice, all who sympathised with the old heathendom, sided with Cnut, and at the end of 1028 Olaf had to take refuge in Russia.

In 1030 Olaf returned, and, crossing Sweden, entered Norway in the Trondhjem region. A battle was fought at Stiklestad, a hamlet near Levanger, at the eastern end of Trondhjem Fjord, on July 29th, 1030. The battle was fierce, and deeds of bravery were done on both sides, but Olaf's little band of faithful men was outnumbered, and at last the king was slain.

With Olaf, as with other great reformers, his death produced a complete revulsion of feeling, which was greatly intensified by a total eclipse of the sun at Stiklestad, a month after the battle. He whom they would not have to rule over them in his life became by his death the nation's saint. Legends soon began to gather round his life and around his death, but something of the spirit of the man has ever since lived on in Norway, and has not been without influence on the great world of Europe.

In the later Saga we read:—

'In the sand-hill where King Olaf's body had lain on the ground a beautiful spring of water came up, and many human ailments and infirmities were cured by its waters. Things were put in order around it, and the water ever since has been carefully preserved. There was first a chapel built, and an altar consecrated, where the king's body had lain; but now Christ's church stands upon the spot. Archbishop Eystein had a high altar raised upon the spot where the king's grave had been, when he erected the great temple which now stands there; and it is the same spot on which the altar of the old Christ Church had stood. It is said that Olaf's church stands on the spot on which the empty house had stood in which King Olaf's body had been laid for the night.'

The traveller who now journeys to Stiklestad will see on the spot where he fell two monuments to Olaf, and hard by a little church that dates back to the century after his death. And those who wander over Trondhjem Cathedral can see in its fine proportions and beautiful workmanship one way in which the affection and gratitude of the succeeding age attempted to do honour to the great king. There were once four, there are still two churches in London named after him.

The annals of Norway are full of interesting men and stirring deeds, but the subject can be pursued here no further. A few pictures only have been dimly outlined of the men whose influence made Norway what she has since been, and who have thus had a powerful influence, first on England, and then through her on the life and thought of the world.

TRONDJHEM CATHEDRAL.

FROM TRONDHJEM TO THE NORTH CAPE.

A Lofoten Village during the Fishing Season.

TRONDHJEM, THE ANCIENT CAPITAL OF NORWAY.

CHAPTER III.

FROM TRONDHJEM TO THE NORTH CAPE.

FIRST IMPRESSIONS OF TRONDHJEM—SUMMER EVENING LIGHT—HISTORY OF THE CATHEDRAL— SUNDAY MORNING SERVICE—THE CHOIR AND OCTAGON—ENVIRONS OF TRONDHJEM—MUNKHOLMEN—THE LERFOS —STEAMBOAT TRAVELLING—CHARACTER OF NORTH-WEST COAST OF NORWAY—MIST AND ITS EFFECTS— TORGHATTEN LEGENDS—THE LOFOTENS—HENNINGSVÆR—THE LOFOTEN FISHERIES—RELIGIOUS WORK AMONGST THE FISHERMEN—THE RAFT SUND—FIRST SIGHT OF THE MIDNIGHT SUN—A WONDERFUL LANDSCAPE—TROMSÖ—THE LAPPS—RELIGIOUS WORK AMONGST THEM—HAMMERFEST—THE SVÆRHOLT-KLUBBEN, OR GREAT BIRD ROCK—THE NORTH CAPE—THE MIDNIGHT SUN—VARDÖ—VADSÖ—THE LYNGEN FJORD.

TRONDHJEM is the oldest and in many respects the most interesting of the important Norwegian cities. The best approach is by steamer up the pleasant Trondhjem Fjord. At the end of a most enjoyable sail, the traveller sees the town spread out before him on the peninsula formed by the Nid, and surrounded by near and distant hills. From afar the eye is attracted by the prominent but not lovely cathedral tower. On reaching the landing-stage at the mouth of the river Nid, or on entering by the less picturesque railway approach, after a preliminary visit to the Britannia Hotel, or Hôtel d'Angleterre, the visitor sallies forth for a stroll through the streets.

These are wide, rectangular, and paved both in the roadway and on the side-walks with round cobble stones, which soon convince the stranger that they do not form the pleasantest of pathways to tread. The houses are for the most part of wood, and are clean and neat-looking, almost every window being adorned with flowers in the summer. The shops are numerous and eminently respectable, for the most part, in appearance; combining an almost entire absence of display with very attractive assortments of goods.

Every stroll in Trondhjem ends either on one of the hills to the east or west of the town, from which very beautiful views are obtained, or in the cathedral precincts. Although the latter building presents a somewhat nondescript and ruinous exterior, yet, seen under the beauty of a Norwegian summer evening, the foliage of the trees, the graveyard, so different from those in England, and the old walls and towers which go back so many centuries, combine to leave a very pleasant and very impressive picture upon the mind. When we first looked upon it, the bright sunset light made it difficult to realise that it was nearly eleven o'clock. But so it was, the night in the month of June consisting of three or four hours of a soft, dreamy, sunset light, combined very frequently with the most exquisite cloud colouring.

One evening, on returning from a visit to a country house a short distance out of the town, at half-past eleven the whole western sky was flooded with a beautiful sapphire light, and after midnight it was still a delight to watch the fairy scene. Even at that early hour many people were about the streets; the afternoon siesta, which every one in Norway appears to take in the summer time, seeming to remove the necessity for a good night's sleep.

A first view of the cathedral usually results—on the part of any who take the least interest in ecclesiastical and historic buildings—in a determination to examine it thoroughly. The structure has a very long architectural history. It owes its existence to the fame and sanctity of Olaf the Saint, whose body, shortly after his death at the battle of Stiklestad, was 'brought to Trondhjem. The remains were soon after transferred to a shrine in St. Clement's Church; and, like that of Becket at Canterbury in the next century, this soon became the object of pilgrimage. Trondhjem became an archbishopric in 1151, and the number of pilgrims necessitated the erection of a more splendid church, the means to do this being supplied by their liberal gifts. Accordingly Eystein, the third archbishop, in 1161 began to build the transept, containing the beautiful chapel of St. John, with its fine Norman arch. Over this, reached by a winding staircase in the wall, is a chapel dedicated to St. Olaf, and filled with a curious collection of fragments brought together from different parts of the cathedral. Eystein also erected the beautiful chapter house.

THORWALDSEN'S STATUE OF THE SAVIOUR.

The present appearance of the transept (1884) is very unimpressive. It is boarded off from the ruined nave to the west, and from the choir to the east, the latter being the most beautiful part of the building. A huge and unsightly organ and singers' loft disfigure the west side of the transept, and prevent the visitor from getting the impression the fine proportions of the transept would otherwise give. Yet, notwithstanding these drawbacks, there is much that favourably impresses the visitor.

The services are conducted in the transept, but, judging from one attended on a Sunday morning, no effort whatever is made to render them specially attractive. The building was filled to its uttermost capacity, and in the singing every one seemed to join. But to the unaccustomed ear it sounded bald and harsh to a degree. The sermon was vigorous, and listened to with interest, but as it *was* 'understanded of the people,' the hearer unskilled in Norse had to possess his soul in patience.

At the south end of the transept is the temporary altar, and there stands a magnificent cast of Thorwaldsen's masterpiece, the grand statue of the Saviour, the glory of the great Fru Kirche in Copenhagen. The eye gladly rested upon this tender, inviting, and yet superhuman figure, expressing in action its inscription: 'Come unto Me, all ye that labour and are heavy-laden, and I will give you rest.' The statue aroused more than passing thoughts of Him who came to 'lay down His life for the sheep,' 'to gather into one the children of God that are scattered abroad,' and who went away that the Comforter might come to guide us into all truth. The ear could not follow the preacher, but that colossal figure, in the dim light of the ancient cathedral, preached a sermon perhaps all the more powerful because it found no articulate expression.

About 1240 the present choir and the far-famed octagon were built. The choir is now in process of restoration, and will be available for use at no distant period. It is a fine

OLD NORSE BOSS,
THE OCTAGON, TRONDHJEM CATHEDRAL.

specimen of the early Gothic, the columns and pointed arches, built of the dark slate-coloured stone of the district, appearing beautiful even amid the scaffolding and the din inseparable from restoration processes. Sixty thousand kronor (about £3600) are being annually spent on this work. So much of the fine detail and carving work remains that the architect confidently expects to leave the choir exactly in appearance as it looked in A.D. 1240.

There is much fine stone carving in the way of bosses and capitals, more especially in and about the octagon, of which some engravings are here given.

To the east of the choir stands the octagon, a light, graceful building of the date of the choir, erected to receive St. Olaf's shrine. It is said to stand on the spot where he was originally buried; and in the south chapel is situated the well containing the spring which is said to have gushed forth in 1030. The silver reliquary which stood for centuries on an altar in the centre of the octagon is said to have weighed two hundred pounds. It was carried off during the Reformation troubles to Copenhagen, and soon disappeared.

Towards the close of the thirteenth century the spacious nave, now a ruin, was built. As soon as the choir is completed, the whole restoration energy will be devoted to rebuilding this. It is beautiful even in its decay; and the west end exterior, even in ruins, as may be seen in the engraving, retains something of its ancient glory.

OLD NORSE CAPITAL,
THE SCREEN, TRONDHJEM CATHEDRAL.

Considering that the cathedral has suffered from at least five fires, during four centuries, the wonder is that any of the edifice has survived to delight the traveller, who little expects, so near to the Arctic Circle, to find a building so rich in architecture and so abundant in historical associations.

The environs of Trondhjem are very picturesque, and capable of affording ever-varying pleasure to the visitor who can afford time to explore them. In the fjord, immediately opposite the town, is the little island of Munkholmen, on which formerly stood one of the oldest monasteries in Northern Europe. When the Swedes besieged Trondhjem, in 1658, the

OLD NORSE CAPITAL,
THE OCTAGON, TRONDHJEM CATHEDRAL.

WEST FRONT, TRONDHJEM CATHEDRAL.

Norwegians fortified the island, and there is now on it a small fortification, pleasing to the eye, but of very slight strength. A massive turret still stands, in all probability the remains of the early monastic building. It has often been used as a dungeon, and from 1680 to 1698, Peter Griffenfeld, the minister of Charles V., was confined here.

A very pleasant way of spending a couple of hours is to hire a boat in the quaint old harbour, row out as far as Munkholmen, and from its grass-grown walls survey the town of Trondhjem spread out before the eye, and the beautiful fjord views, all seen to perfection under the brilliant light of a June afternoon.

A mile or two from Trondhjem is the village of Lade, where dwelt the last powerful heathen jarl, who was conquered by Olaf Tryggveson.

A few miles inland are two considerable waterfalls, called the Greater and Lesser Lerfos. They are easily reached either on foot or by carriage, and, though unable to compare with many that Norway can show, are yet well worth a visit.

Trondhjem is the great centre for the Nordland and Northern Norway. The country people come in from miles round for supplies; the town is the

THE LESSER LERFOS, NEAR TRONDHJEM.
From a photograph by Mr. G. H. Hodges.

northern limit for many travellers who, having come on by rail from Christiania, go back either by way of Molde and Bergen, or *viâ* Storlien to Stockholm. The North Cape steamers all touch here, and Trondhjem is the natural starting-place for the extreme north.

Along the west coast of Norway the steamboat by necessity takes the place of the railway. A worse country for railways could hardly be imagined. But as the steamers at almost every part of their route sail between the fringe of rocky islets and the mainland, where the water is nearly always smooth, no pleasanter mode of travel can be conceived. The traveller sits in comfortable chairs under well-spread awnings, or lounges idly over the bulwarks, while he is borne past an ever-changing panorama of distant snow-clad mountains; rocky islands, sometimes bleak and bare, sometimes clothed in the most beautiful foliage; up fairy-like fjords with tiny villages dotted here and there on the shore; and this in a land where it seems 'always afternoon,' and where midnight differs from mid-day only in the fact that the heat is less oppressive, and the light more beautiful.

The officers of the steamers speak English fluently, the table is well kept, and affords a variety of diet not always attainable inland, and the berths are at least as comfortable as the curious beds peculiar to the older Norwegian stations.

There is a regular mail service from Hamburgh to Vadsö, and steamers start twice or thrice a week from Trondhjem to the North Cape. These call at all the considerable villages on the way up and down, to take on board or to land both passengers and cargo. But during the last year or two the increase in the travellers has been so great that the two chief steamboat companies for six weeks in the summer fit up their newest and most commodious vessels solely for the accommodation of those who wish to see the North Cape and intervening coast scenery. No steerage passengers or cargo are carried, and the vessels call only at those parts which are of exceptional beauty or interest.

At midnight on June 21st, 1884, we left Trondhjem in one of the best of these steamers, the Sverre Sigurdsson, for the far-distant northernmost point of Europe. The Nid Elv runs with a swift current, necessitating care as the steamer, about 1000 tons in size, warps slowly out of the narrow harbour. We watched the town as it gradually receded and finally was hid from sight by a projecting headland, and then, having previously seen the fjord, turned in about 1 A.M., in order to be up betimes the next morning to see the celebrated coast scenery near the Arctic Circle.

The voyage along the north-west coast of Norway in one of the North Cape steamers carries the traveller through an apparently endless succession of straits and fjords, dotted with numberless rocky islets. Views of great beauty and interest are always to be seen, and here and there on the route scenes and objects of peculiar interest occur. Much of course depends upon the state of the atmosphere. With fine weather the trip is perfection; and even with cloudy and misty weather compensations come in the way of extraordinary landscape effects.

For instance, when on the journey referred to above, we reached the deck early in the next morning, the sun was shining brilliantly, bathing with fresh morning light the near rocks and the distant mountains, the narrow strait through which we were sailing, and the parts of the great Atlantic we could see through openings in the rocky barrier. But away behind us was a cloud, not much 'bigger than a man's hand,' that at first appeared to be stationary, but that soon, to our disquiet, was perceived to be in rapid chase of the steamer. Up it came, faster and faster, until in ten or fifteen minutes the ocean, islands and mountains were all hidden from view. The anchor was dropped, and dismay sat upon every countenance. We had a quiet—unusually quiet—breakfast; and, after idly swinging at anchor for an hour, the steamer began slowly to feel her way north again. Dismal stories were told of friends who had been to the North Cape and back without catching a

TORGHATTEN FROM THE EAST.
(*From a sketch by Professor T. G. Bonney.*)

glimpse of the sun the whole way. The fog lifted, but it continued thick and misty most of the day. Yet there were compensations. Every now and then a huge glacier or snow-field would become visible, high up above the clouds, borne up seemingly in some mysterious way upon them. Mountain peaks acquired unfamiliar and grotesque forms, and the whole landscape seemed to gain a weird charm that atoned in some small measure for the loss of the sun.

We had a somewhat similar morning when much further north, and then also the occasional glimpses of mountains and ice-fields cut off apparently from all connection with the earth, and consequently appearing much loftier than they were, was very impressive.

The first object of exceptional interest on the journey north is Torghatten, the famous mountain with the hole through it. A coast like the Norwegian could hardly fail to lead to the origination of legends; and the explanation of the aperture in Torghatten is characteristic. A giant and giantess, who fell in love during a casual meeting at a friend's, had to part at length, and did so with the usual lovers' vows. The giantess had returned home to nurse her sick brother, who at first promised that she should marry her lover, but who afterwards desired her to marry one of his dissolute friends. The special family gift in this instance was the power of petrifaction, and the brother turned into various rocky islets the messengers sent by the lover to his mistress. The lover's peculiar faculty was the power of hitting everything he shot at, and at last, getting into a great rage at what he thought was his mistress's faithlessness, he shot an arrow at her, although he was only seventy miles away. The wicked brother happened to be bathing at the time, and as it was very wet he wore his hat. The arrow went through both hat and skull, and then fell at the feet of the lady. She loved her brother in spite of his faults, and in her despair also used the family gift, and turned herself into stone at Lecko, her brother at Torghatten, and her lover on horseback at Hestmando.

THE NATURAL TUNNEL THROUGH TORGHATTEN.

The legendary explanations will hardly be considered final in these days, and no generally accepted scientific theory has yet been formulated. But it certainly is a most curious and interesting phenomenon. At one point between the island and the mainland the light through the hole can be seen from the deck of the steamer. The mountain is about eight hundred feet high, and the cavern, which is about half-way up, is reached by an easy climb. The view looking through the cavern is very fine. The tunnel is about a hundred yards long, and from sixty to a hundred feet high.

Farther north we pass the Seven Sisters, a bold and striking range of mountains; and just where we cross the Arctic Circle the Hestmando comes into view.

After passing Bodo the scenery on the mainland reaches its highest point of savage grandeur, and the steamer sails past the precipitous island of Lendogarde and across the great Vest Fjord to the Lofoten Islands. It is here, if anywhere, that the vessel is apt to catch Neptune in one of his restless moods. On leaving the mainland the Lofotens appear first as a great wall rising up on the distant horizon. They are full forty miles distant, although, owing to the clearness of the atmosphere, it is hard to believe that they are so far away. On nearer approach the wall resolves itself into a large number of jagged mountain peaks and precipices 2000 to 3000 feet high. The passages between the islands are very narrow and tortuous, and the scenery unique. As the steamer draws near these fantastic and imposing heights no passage appears navigable to the untrained eye. Sometimes through a narrow strait, sometimes through inlets that seem perilously con-

HENNINGSVÆR.

tracted, sometimes by turning right angles of rock, the vessel begins to thread her way among the islands.

The first Lofoten village we saw was Henningsvær, the centre of the great Lofoten cod fishery. The houses are scattered over some small islets nestled at the foot of the Vaagekelle (pronounced Võgĕkellĕ), which to the eye appears about 1200 feet high, but which is given by the authorities as 3090 feet.

In all mountainous districts in Norway it is difficult to estimate heights, since the mountains mainly consist of plateaus rather than isolated peaks, and the atmosphere is so clear that an eye accustomed to judge distance by English or Scotch atmospheres is constantly at fault. Even after considerable experience it is hard to believe that some cliff is ten miles off when it

A FINLAND FISHING BOAT.

appears to be at the most but three. It is only the logic of fact, and the careful observation of the time taken by the steamer to reach it, that convinces the sceptical.

Henningsvær presents an attractive picture from the steamer, but, like so many of the Nordland villages, does not bear close inspection so well. The evidences of the fishing industry are very manifest to both sight and smell. From February until April each year cod-fishing is pursued with great vigour in all the Lofoten region. A notion of the importance of this industry may be gained from the following figures. The boats come from all parts of Norway, and many even from Finland. From 25,000 to 30,000 men and 6000 to 7000 boats are employed in the fishery. In 1881 as many as 28,400,000 cod were caught. The cod come to this region every year to spawn. They are caught with long lines like those used by English cod-liners in the North Sea; by nets and by hand-lines.

The fish are also cured in three ways: first, being split open, the backbone removed, and quickly dried in the open air; second, being opened, salted, and dried on the rocks; third, opened, tied two together, and dried on frames. Great quantities of fish drying in this way are commonly seen in different parts of North Norway. The dried fish is exported chiefly to Italy and Spain, and consumed there. Cod-liver oil is also extensively manufactured, and the heads are made into a manure.

The whole fishing arrangements are under Government control; drinking is prohibited, and a chaplain is stationed in the islands during the season, and much is done for the religious welfare of the men engaged. It is a rough, hard life, and Christian work there is not at all easy, nor always so successful as the labourers could wish. Here is an extract from a recent report of the Home Missions and Colportage Society of Norway. The colporteur writes:—

'Putting my trust in God, and praying for His help, I started from home. After some difficulties I reached the district of my labours. The weather continued equally bad. It was only with the utmost difficulty that one could save one's own life and property on dry land, and if attempts occasionally were made to get out at sea, the nets were lost and no fish was got. Complaints were heard of losses at home, losses on journeys, losses of boats and nets. Discouragement and despondency—nay, even loud-voiced grumbling against the Lord and His dispensation—one met with on all sides. The expectation that the grave language of the elements might serve as a means in the hand of God to melt the obstinate heart of man was painfully disappointed, and it was grievous to witness how, on the contrary, the people went farther in stiff-necked resistance, closing their hearts in defiance of God. They became more confirmed in hardening their hearts. None would listen to what I said. "If God were good, as you say," they answered me, "He would still the tempest and send fish under land, so that we should not have to prepare for want and hunger." The room was dreadfully crowded, and far into the night swearing and quarrels from the card game were heard all around me.

'It is a hard task to live and work among such a company. God knows how many hard hours I have had on my wandering from one fishing-booth to another, and more than once I have had to go aside and ask of my Father in heaven patience, wisdom, and words that might reach the hearts of the people. I found that He is a God that will hear prayers. He gave me greater frankness and confidence of heart, ability to answer the discontent that made itself heard, and power of awakening doubting and

THE RAFT SUND.

irresolute minds to the consciousness that our own sins are the cause of our sufferings, and that we ought to thank God that He, while it is yet the time of mercy, tries as well by His love as by His chastisement to bring us to consciousness of our sins, and opens His arms to all repentant sinners, so that it behoves us not to refuse the gracious offer now. But I found, I am glad to say, also many Christians, who, with prayer and reliance in their dear God and Father, thanked Him for the chastisement. To these my visits seemed to afford great consolation and encouragement, and many a blessed hour was spent in the boats among these.'

Now and then, as in our own North Sea trawling, great and lamentable loss of life takes place from the sudden and violent storms that arise.

Leaving Henningsvær, we entered the Gimsö Strom, a narrow strait with bold precipitous hills on each side. Dwarf trees flourish near the water's edge, mosses of various kinds higher up the slopes, but the higher ridges are bare rock, covered in many places with snow, presenting a wild and eerie appearance. A long afternoon's sail past the west coast of Ost Vaago, and then a sudden turn at almost right angles through a most beautiful and picturesque little strait, brought the steamer into the Raft Sund. For nearly two hours we sailed through this narrow winding passage, at once the most characteristic and the most striking scene in the Lofotens. The water-way is very narrow, and the mountains on either side rise abruptly from the sea. In whatever direction the eye turns, it rests upon wonderful masses of mountain peaks of all conceivable shapes, barren and bleak, with large patches of snow wherever crevices or sufficiently level spaces allow it to lodge. The charm of the scene is its variety and completeness. The steamer sails through the clear smooth green water; nestling along the shore wherever a little level space can be found are the huts of the fishermen; the lower slopes are bright with the foliage of dwarf trees, the higher slopes with Alpine mosses; the upper cliffs and peaks are either rocks of the most forbidding kind or brilliant snow masses; and over all is the clear sky, against which the fantastic pinnacles stand out in the boldest relief. In passing from the hamlet at the foot of the mountain to the awe-inspiring precipices at the top, the eye seems to traverse at a glance over the whole scale of Nature, from her most attractive to her most forbidding phase.

Rounding the south-east corner of the large island of Hindö, the journey north is resumed, passing the sheltered little hamlet of Lodingen. Here a small boat came off with a telegram for one of our passengers, and it was a kind of mental shock to realise that away north, well within the Arctic Circle, we were still in easy communication with London.

The evening that followed is never likely to be forgotten by those who witnessed its splendour from the deck of the Sverre Sigurdsson. As we sailed along the east coast of Hindö and through the Tjall Sund, the clouds which had been hanging about all the afternoon began to clear away. In the soft evening light the near and distant mountains formed views of beauty unimagined. The captain had so timed our sailing that by midnight we were to be well out in the Vaags Fjord, off Harstadhavn, where could be seen, without the interposition of any mountain barrier, the midnight sun, if he deigned to show himself.

As midnight drew near, the scene became one of entrancing loveliness. We were steaming up a broad fjord wherein the water was perfectly smooth, and which was completely enclosed by mountain landscapes, except in the direction of the sun. An indescribably beautiful crimson light flooded the whole landscape, so that one seemed to be looking through a mysteriously beautiful medium upon some fairy scene. There was a wonderful stillness over all nature, and a great silence that was not without its effect upon the traveller. The sun slowly descended below some bars of deep purple cloud, and a few minutes before midnight the full-orbed disc shone out clear and distinct a few degrees above the horizon.

Flooded in the pinkish crimson light lay a landscape that surpassed all description. In front stretched the open waters of one of Norway's most lovely fjords; to the left was the little village of Harstadhavn, built in a

TROMSÖ.

semicircular valley, the many trim houses, the little port, and the old Throndenæs Church giving it an appearance of solidity and comfort; opening up behind the village was a fertile, tree-clad valley, branching out into two arms that gradually merged into nearer hills; and forming a grand semicircular background was a lofty range of snow-capped mountains. Even while we gazed, the crimson light changed, the sun began to mount in the sky, the solemn hush passed away, and all nature looked fresh and gay in the bright white morning light. It was almost impossible to realise that it was 12.30 A.M.

Early the next morning we reached Tromsö, the great port of the Nordland. Here the autumn herring fishery has its head-quarters, and here vessels fit out for expeditions into the Polar Sea. The little town is well situated along the eastern slope of a hilly island on the shore of the Tromsö Sund. It is compact and well built, containing from five to six thousand inhabitants. Above the town, higher up the slope, are fine groves of birch-trees, and across the Sund is the Tromsödal, up which, at a distance of two or three miles, is the Lapp encampment.

There are a few good shops at Tromsö, but on the whole intending purchasers will find it better to depend on the more extensive supplies of Trondhjem or Bergen. The harbour is generally lively with the coast steamers and numerous vessels connected either with the Hamburgh or Russian trade; but to the north and south snow-clad mountains shut in the view.

LAPP HUT.

The trip to the so-called Lapp encampment is a pleasant one. The Sund is crossed either in the steamer's boats or in one of the many plying about for hire. For those not equal to a short walk ponies can be engaged. The path follows the course of a little stream and leads through clumps of birch-trees. On either side the hills rise abruptly, and here and there large patches of snow are to be seen.

The encampment itself strikes a stranger as something of a delusion. It is true that there are one or two wretched huts, presumably of the kind that the Lapp in his native state professes to dwell in; but we were somewhat amused to find that the Lapps we had tramped two or three miles to observe were no other than a group whose countenances and ways we had previously studied when they were idling at the end of Tromsö's main street.

LAPP CRADLE.

As it was somewhat early in the summer they had perhaps not been able to tear themselves away from civilisation, and certainly the lee-side of a house in Tromsö is, if anything, better quarters than the huts built after the Lapp model.

It was in Tromsö also, and not at the encampment, that we were able to study the Lapp method of managing babies. The main idea seems to be so to secure the infant that if the mother is compelled to leave it she may reasonably expect to find her offspring safe on her return. The little one is laced into a cradle, made of wooden ribs covered with leather, in such a manner that it is impossible to fall out. As far as we could see, the infant is expected to spend most of his early years in a cradle like that represented on page 65. They are perhaps easier to handle than an infant possessing free use of its limbs, and they are well adapted to be put down at short notice and in rough places. On the string stretched from one end to the other, beads or glittering objects are strung to amuse the infant. By a strap attached to both ends the mother slings it over her shoulder when walking, and when she wishes to work hangs it up, if need be, upon a tree. We thought we could see that amid all the seemingly rough and—for the infant—trying habits of the Lapp parent, there are motherly affections. It was another instance of how 'one touch of nature makes the whole world kin.'

But the Lapps at the encampment had done what they could for the entertainment of their visitors. They had driven down from the fjeld a small herd of reindeer, but not including, unfortunately, the monarchs of the flock, with their long, wide-spreading antlers. It is, perhaps, impossible to over-estimate the value of this animal to the Lapps. In the full vigour of life the males act as beasts of burden, especially in winter, drawing their owners over the snow-slopes in the curious sledge which represents the height of Lapp inventiveness in the department of locomotion. The females supply the milk which is not only an important article of diet, but from which also large quantities of cheese are made. The Lapp rarely slaughters the reindeer for food until it is beginning to grow old and feeble, but when that stage is reached he utilises the flesh for food and the skin for raiment and for foot-coverings. Tending the herds of reindeer takes up a large part of the working life of a Lapp; and hence, as wealth, as an end in life, as food and raiment, and as a means of locomotion, the reindeer plays an important part in Lapland life.

In addition to providing the small herd of reindeer, the Tromsö Lapps had also set up, beside two very dreary and dismal huts that seem to be in permanent occupation of that part of the valley, a tent arranged after the fashion of their abodes when in the full exercise of their nomadic propensities. Before this they spread reindeer skins, which they offered for sale, also spoons made by a very rough process out of reindeer horn. They were persuaded by friendly and pecuniary considerations to allow themselves to be photographed, and we are enabled to exhibit the result, although we grieve to have to state that the dog who looks so peaceful in the engraving paid attentions of a too personal nature to the photographer during the preliminary arrangements. The picture gives a fair notion of the typical features and appearance. The

Herd of Reindeer in Lapland.

Lapps are generally small in stature and of a preternaturally aged and wrinkled countenance. Even the children look like patriarchs, and the men, from their diminutive size, might easily be mistaken for children, were it not for the grave and worn cast of face which they invariably exhibit.

As it is only at Tromsö that many travellers in Norway touch this strange and interesting race, a few words about them may not here be out

LAPPS IN TROMSDAL.
(From a photograph by Mr. G. H. Hodges.)

of place. Lapland extends over the northern parts of Norway and Sweden, and over the north-western part of Russia. The origin of the race is very obscure; the most probable explanation is that they came from Finland, but do not spring from the Finnish stock. There is a certain resemblance to the Finns both in language and habits, but the differences are so considerable that it seems more reasonable to conclude that the Lapps represent an earlier race conquered by the Finns. The most probable etymology of the name seems to be that it comes from a Finnish word *lappu*, meaning 'land's-end

SWEDISH LAPLANDERS.

folk' or exiles. For a long period past there has been constant intercourse between the two races; but the Finns are a finer set of men physically.

They are taller and stronger, and better fitted for industrial labour. In Sweden they greatly outnumber the Lapps, there being about 15,000 of them as against 7000 Lapps. In Norway this is reversed, the Lapps numbering 16,000 or 17,000, the Finns about 8000.

The Norwegian Lapps consist of the nomad or Mountain Lapps, the settled or Sea Lapps, and the River Lapps. The second is the most numerous class. A large amount of interesting information about the Lapp people and their habits has been given by Mr. Sophus Tromholt, a member of the International Polar Research Expedition of 1882–83, in his recently published (1885) work, *Under the Rays of the Aurora Borealis*. We venture to give a few extracts from his entertaining book, the latest and one of the best on the subject. 'The Mountain Lapps,' he says, 'are the parent tribe of the two other varieties of the same race. To the mountain, the desert, to the life in the free open air, the very existence of the nomad Lapps is closely allied. The Lapp passes almost his entire life in the open air, and his tent does not even protect him against the autumn rain, the winter snow, or the spring storms. Sometimes the rain floods his tent, or the snow envelopes, and sometimes the wind levels it with the ground. But still the snowy desert is his chosen home, and it is only here that he can be studied and judged with justice. The roaming life of the nomad of North Europe over the free mountains and the snowy wastes, where he may pitch his tent and graze his reindeer where he lists, free from the trammels of civilisation, in constant fight with the elements, calls to life and fosters a sense of independence and strength which undoubtedly has the effect of making him contented. In summer as in winter, in spring and in fall, the Mountain Lapp roams over the immense high plateau with his reindeer herd, guarding it day and night. With this he is brought up: it forms his sole heirloom. His father was a nomad, as were also his ancestors before him. In order to maintain and increase his herd the Lapp has to toil and suffer like the peasant on his inherited patch of soil.'

The Mountain Lapps in summer visit the sea-shore because the reindeer roam there to cooler quarters, and that they may bathe in the sea. By the absence of the animals during the summer the moss is allowed to grow more richly on the higher regions for the winter pasturage.

The reindeer is the Lapp horse, and the sledge, though not constructed according to civilised notions, is yet found by experience to be skilfully adapted to the conditions of the country. Mr. Tromholt's description is full of interest: 'The travelling requisites are as simple as they can be. First, two symmetrically-shaped bits of wood are laid above and below the neck of the deer, and fastened together. From the middle of these a band runs down on each side to a semicircular wooden block under the stomach, immediately behind the fore-legs. To this block the single trace is also attached, which is at the other end run through the fore-part of the *pulk* or sledge. Around the neck a rope or band is laid, from the lower point of which the rein runs. This is a single one, and the end is wound several times round the right wrist of the driver, the thumb having previously been inserted in a hole in the end of the rein. The sleigh seems from its construction to be better adapted to water than land travelling. Cut a low boat in halves, take the stem part and close it behind with a perpendicular sheet of wood, and you have a pulk. It is about the length of a man, without any covering whatever, and completely empty, the driver squatting down in the bottom. As it is provided with a keel, it is about as easily managed as a boat on *terra firma*. The pulk is built of birch-wood, but the keel, four to six inches wide, and finishing in a point in front, is of fir.'

The advantages of this vehicle as compared with a sledge on two runners are: 'A sleigh would sink far deeper into loose snow, and be knocked to pieces over rough ground where the road is obstructed with logs and stones, and the pulk has often to shoot down a declivity of a couple of yards. The sleigh would capsize quicker than the pulk, strange as it may seem, as the latter only capsizes in the hands of an inexperienced driver. The expert, however, has it completely in his power, and understands how to keep it straight with his body in places where a sleigh would be hopelessly upset.'

Mr. Tromholt gives a vivid picture of his first experience behind a reindeer. 'I imagined it would not be unlike driving with horses or bullocks. At the last moment somebody kindly gave me a few hints as to the placing of my body. I got inside, wound the rein around my wrist, and, before I had even time to think or look ahead, the whole caravan shot forward, and off we went in the wildest and most chaotic manner, without order, right and left, the pulks swaying to and fro, and see-sawing by way of variety on their keels. I knew enough to understand that the secret of pulk-driving was to stick to the vehicle. I therefore let reindeer be reindeer, and did my best to accommodate myself to the pitching of the pulk by all the arts of balancing, and, although I am at a loss to understand how, I managed to keep my seat.'

The Lapps are a peaceful and inoffensive people, untouched to any appreciable extent by modern influences. They wander after the reindeer now much as their forefathers did when Harold Fairhair placed all Norway under his sway. They have long had a reputation for magic, and, according to their own dim traditions, sprang originally from the East. They have been oppressed at various times in the past, but seem now free from the risk of that extinction which so often comes upon subject-races of a low type of civilisation.

A great deal has been done for them, both from an educational and from a religious point of view. Gustavus Adolphus took a great interest in their development, building both churches and schools, and providing funds for

Sunday in Lapland.

their maintenance. The Scriptures were translated into their tongue, and tracts and books prepared for them. Many of the natives were trained as missionaries, whose labours bore fruit, although in such a nomadic, scattered people the old heathen beliefs and practices lingered on for a long while.

Lapp congregations in the far north have to come either on the long bone snow-shoes, or in the reindeer sledges, many miles over the snow-covered ice-bound roads, to the churches established and supported by the State for their benefit. In many districts the clergyman is in residence only during the winter, and occasionally the funerals, baptisms, weddings, and religious services for the year are all crowded into a small space of time.

Mr. Tromholt thus describes a Sunday service in Lapland : 'The church is quite crowded. In the middle is the oven, and on one side the men are seated, on the other the women. The Lapp verger steps forth from the vestry door, and reads the lessons in the tongue of his forefathers. He then calls out the number of the Psalm in the Lapp prayer-book, and initiates the singing; only a few members of the congregation join in it, and their contribution does not add to the harmony. The sermon is generally read in Norwegian and interpreted by the verger, or by some able Lapp. The vicars do not stay long enough in these inhospitable parts to learn Lappish thoroughly, and, on the other hand, few Lapps understand Norwegian. As the service is drawing to a close, crying, sighs, wails, and even shrieks may be heard from the female part of the congregation, but they generally emanate from old women. It is, however, very characteristic of the Lapps that they are, now perhaps less than formerly, given to strong religious emotions which may at times assume the form of a fanatical frenzy.'

We give on the opposite page an illustration of a Sunday service in Lapland, of which the following is a description :—

'The Mountain Lapps arrived attired in their warm fur coats made of reindeer skins. They had their dogs with them; the deer that had been drawing their sledges were fastened some distance off. They had brought skins with them as well as reindeer meat, which they wanted to barter or sell to the traders, for after the service is over it is like a market—brisk trade is carried on. The church bells were beginning to ring, summoning the people to the sacred building. The Laplanders began slowly (for they are never very quick in their movements) to go across to the church. The church is a wooden structure with a spire; all the seats are painted yellow, and the walls whitewashed. There was a neat little pulpit and altar; above the latter was an oil-painting of our Saviour in Gethsemane, and I was astonished to find so superior a work of art in those cold desolate regions, in latitude 71°.

'The little church was nearly filled. A Sea Lapp, apparently of superior rudimentary education, gave out the hymn in a loud voice. The pastor now mounted the pulpit, and began his sermon in the Lapp *lingua*. The congregation listened very attentively; but after ten minutes or so some of them went out for a little time; it was very cold sitting still. The sermon being over, two couples, followed by bridesmaids and best men, went up to the altar, to go through the wedding ceremony. After the conclusion of the marriages all the people went to the school-house, and everybody was welcome to the feast.'

After leaving Tromsö the steamer sails on hour after hour through narrow sounds, across wide fjords, in the clear light of the unending Arctic Circle day, and past an ever-varying succession of islands and mountains

HAMMERFEST HARBOUR.
(*From a photograph by Mr. G. H. Holges.*)

and hamlets, the latter few and far between. At length Hammerfest, the most northerly town in Europe, is reached, and is seen to be a well-built compact little place, consisting mainly of one street running parallel with part of the harbour. It seems largely given over to the manufacture of cod-liver oil, a fact soon discovered by the visitor. The houses are of wood, and look neat and fairly clean. The harbour shows signs of considerable trade, and is fringed with picturesque old warehouses. The inhabitants number from 2000 to 3000. There is here, as in all Norwegian towns and villages, a good school. Articles of Lapp manufacture, walrus-tusks and Lapp dresses, are to be had, though not in any great abundance. Hammerfest also possesses scientific associations. Many of the Arctic explorers have touched there. Sir Edward Sabine conducted some of his experiments on the

pendulum here in 1823; and there stands on a conspicuous knoll near the harbour the *Meridianstötte*, a stone pillar erected in commemoration of the measurement of the degrees of latitude between Ismail, near the mouth of the Danube, and Hammerfest. From the Tyven, a hill to the south of the town 1230 feet high, a good view of the island on which Hammerfest stands, and of the Arctic Ocean, is obtained.

North of Hammerfest the scenery becomes less imposing, but more drear and barren. The North Cape is on the island separated from the mainland of Europe by the Magerö Sund. Passing through this sound, and across the mouth of the great Porsanger Fjord, which runs

THE SVÆRHOLTKLUBBEN, OR BIRD ROCK.
(*From a photograph by Mr. G. H. Hodges.*)

for about eighty miles inland in a southerly direction, one of the great natural curiosities in the Arctic Circle comes into view. This is the Sværholt-klubben, a huge cliff about 1200 feet high, and half a mile wide, which has been from time immemorial the resort of enormous numbers of gulls and other sea-fowl. On all the ledges and in all the crevices of the rocks, from the sea-level to the top of the cliff, these birds build their nests. As the steamer sails abreast of the cliff, thousands are seen flying about, uttering their shrill cries, or else sitting in rows along all the ledges. When opposite

THE NORTH CAPE.

the centre of the cliff the steam whistle is blown vigorously, and almost instantly the face of the cliff becomes white with flapping gulls' wings, and a cloud of gulls, numbering tens upon tens of thousands, fly slowly off to the eastward, gleaming dazzlingly white in the bright sunlight. Their absence seems but slightly to diminish the total number; and successive whistles start successive flights, that wheel slowly and, judging from the tone of their plaintive cries, somewhat reproachfully over the steamer.

Just beyond the cliff is a small station. On the occasion of our visit, a man and a girl came off in a boat, bringing supplies of milk and a basket of gulls' eggs. The latter, intended for the table, were for the most part blown, and carried at least part of the way home as mementoes of a very interesting afternoon in the far north.

The scenery around the Sværholt Rock is full of interest. Away in the distance to the east is Nordkyn, the real northernmost point of the mainland of Europe. To the north-west is the North Cape, reached after a few hours' sail. The vessel is anchored off the very steep ascent by which the top of the cliff, about one thousand feet high, is reached. We landed on Midsummer night, the sea being perfectly still, the sky perfectly clear. The snow had only very recently melted, and the path was damp and slippery in places. We landed in the ship's boats, and our company, about fifty in number, struggled up the steep ascent, reaching the top about 11 P.M. It is a level, stony upland, as dreary and desolate a spot as can well be imagined. The storms of countless ages have worn the cliffs facing north and west into imposing forms, but they seem to have brought the top of the cliff into a dull uniform level. There is nothing picturesque in the landscape. It is bare and barren to a degree that renders it almost oppressive. In all directions the eye can rest upon only wind-swept rocks, or the seemingly limitless ocean. Behind is a wilderness, before, the Polar Sea. On the top of the Cape is the obelisk erected in commemoration of the visit of Oscar II. in 1873, and we reached it shortly before midnight. Away in front of us lay the Arctic Ocean, with the surface perfectly smooth and unruffled; behind us, as far as the eye could see, stretched the bleak, barren uplands. The sun was high in the heavens, at an elevation of 12° to 15° above the horizon, and shining brilliantly as it does about half-past six on a June evening in lower latitudes. Just before midnight a slight crimson or reddish light appeared, a faint suspicion, as it were, of coming sunset, but not to be compared for beauty and impressiveness with the fairy light that flooded the landscape at Harstadhavn.

It was a moment of great interest. As midnight drew near the members of the party collected around the obelisk. In our company were included many nationalities—Norway, Sweden, Denmark, Germany, England, Scotland, and the United States were all well represented. From widely scattered homes and by widely different routes we had been brought together for a few moments on the northernmost spot in Europe. When the sun reached his lowest point, the whistle of the steamer a thousand feet below told us that it was midnight. We behaved as such gatherings on such occasions generally do. We built a cairn; we left a flag flying; we sang 'God save the Queen,' 'My country, 'tis of thee,' and 'Auld lang syne'; we cheered Her Majesty, the President of the United States, and the King of Norway and Sweden, and the captain and officers of the Sverre Sigurdsson, who had so skilfully guided the ship through very intricate and dangerous channels, and whose unfailing courtesy added so much to the interest and pleasure of the voyage.

Even at the North Cape we were not without a reminder that science is ever with us. One of our party had brought up his camera, and had taken one or two photographs, when the idea of having a group taken was mooted. We were all hastily summoned, and, arranging ourselves without premeditation about the obelisk, were speedily possessed of the unique distinction of having been photographed on the top of the North Cape by the light of the midnight sun. An engraving of a part of the group is here given.

The descent was steep and more trying than the ascent, but we reached the steamer about 2 A.M., with the satisfaction of feeling that, owing to the brilliant weather, our expedition had been a great success. There are, it is true, many spots from which the midnight sun may be seen to more advantage, from the point of view of the picturesque, than from the North Cape. And yet, standing upon that eerie, weather-worn upland, the experience is unique. Behind is Europe, with all its diversities of race, with its seething masses of humanity, with its great capitals, its business, its passions, its toil and its cares. In front is the calm, slowly heaving ocean, possessing to the eye no limit, and known to possess no shore but those masses of ice hitherto impervious to all that human skill and courage and endurance can effect. And high in the heavens, the sight of its circuit impeded by no islands or mountains, the eye can watch unobstructed the successive revolutions of the sun through the long weeks of the Arctic day. It is one of the spots which, when visited, photograph themselves for ever on the memory and become one of the happy and inseparable associations of life. Most travellers make the North Cape the turning-point, but the ordinary coasting steamers pursue their voyage to Vadsö. It is an open question whether there is enough new interest in the scenery to compensate for the time expended in getting to the little town that occupies the extreme north-eastern corner of Norway. Nordkyn, the real extremity of Europe, is seen to advantage,

PART OF A GROUP TAKEN AT MIDNIGHT, JUNE 25TH, 1884.
(From a photograph by Mr. G. H. Hodges.)

and is hardly less interesting than the North Cape itself. The snow lies in masses here much nearer to the sea level. Myriads of gulls and auks and other aquatic birds abound, and occasionally huge shoals of fish. But there is a monotony about the scenery, and an absence of human life, that tends to depress the spirits.

Vardo is situated at the extreme north-eastern corner of Norway, in latitude 70° 22', on a little island separated from the mainland by a narrow strait. It contains about one thousand four hundred inhabitants, and, having

VARDO.

two good harbours, is a place of some importance in connection with the Arctic fisheries. It possesses many *Hjelder*, or places for drying fish. The town is not too far north to escape from military influences, and is protected by a fort called the Vardohus, which dates as far back as 1310. It is of no strategic importance in these days, and is garrisoned by a corporal's guard, but it is said that Norway acquired Finmarken by means of this fortress and its garrison. Like so many Norwegian towns, its most conspicuous architectural feature is its wooden church.

Sailing onwards south by west, for about seventy miles, the Norwegian steamboat mail and coasting route comes to an end in the little town of Vadsö. It possesses also Lapp, Russian, and Finnish names, all meaning the same thing, viz., 'water island.' Out of 1700 inhabitants, 900, much the larger half, are Finns. It is wholly given over to the fisheries and allied industries. The frames for drying fish are to be seen on every side, and the occupation of the town is made known far and wide by the odours it sends forth. An interesting spot to visit is the establishment connected

VADSÖ.

with the whale fishery, carried on by means of shooting harpoons into the fish from a cannon on the deck of the steamer. One hundred whales per annum are said to be captured in this way.

As the North Cape steamers do not always time their trips so as to reach every striking part of this wonderful coast at the time most convenient for seeing it, passengers generally on the return journey strive to be on deck when passing the points of interest missed on the upward route. In our case, on the homeward journey we visited the Lyngenfjord, one of the most superb natural glories of Norway. It runs for twenty or thirty miles in a south-easterly direction, and it is walled in by a most imposing series of huge mountains from 5000 to 6000 feet high. From all of these mountains, filling up every valley, huge glaciers descend in many cases almost to the water's edge. Frequently in one noble view the eye can range over gigantic cliffs, over and down the faces of which waterfalls are rushing, the clear blue icy masses stretching along their tops as far as sight can reach. Seen, as we looked upon it, enveloped in mist and rain-

THE SEVEN SISTERS.

clouds, the views were very impressive, and must be vastly more so when the sunlight brings out the wonderful light and shade of the mountains, and the ever-varying colours of fjord, cliffs, glacier and sky.

Further south still we steamed up to the head of the Mel Fjord, and looked upon the mighty masses of the great Svartisen glacier, which here come down to the sea level, and which are estimated to cover over five hundred square miles.

We also had a fine view in the evening light of the Seven Sisters, a range of mountain peaks about 3000 feet high, attractively varied in size and shape, but which can only be made seven to the uninitiated on the principle of the little girl in Wordsworth's 'We are Seven,' viz., by counting in those that are not there.

We bade farewell to the Arctic Circle just as the midnight sun broke through the clouds to give us a parting glimpse of his welcome face, and Hestmando looked more than ever like the horseman wrapped in his cloak, and on a journey to his true love in the distant south.

The next day the hours passed pleasantly by as the steamer bore us past a constant succession of attractive landscapes, and at length once again we looked upon the mouth of the Nid and the tower of St. Olaf's Church.

HESTMANDO.
(*From a sketch by Professor T. G. Bonney.*)

FROM CHRISTIANIA TO THE ROMSDAL.

Interior of an old Thelemarken House now at Bygdø, near Christiania.

CHRISTIANIA.

CHAPTER IV.

From Christiania to the Romsdal.

Christiania Fjord—Carl Johans Gade—The Viking's Ship—A State Funeral.—Sketch of Hans Niel. Hauge—Akers Hus—Oscar's Hall—Frogner Saeter—Lake Mjosen—The Guddrandsdal—The Romsdal.

BY far the larger number of visitors to Norway enter and leave the country *viâ* Christiania, the present capital. The town dates only from 1624, and is named after its founder, Christian IV. An ancient town, Oslo by name, founded by Harald Hardraade about the middle of the eleventh century, occupied what is now the eastern suburb of the city. Like all other Norwegian cities, it has suffered much from fire, notably in the years 1686, 1706 and 1858. The result has been to give the city a modern, well-built appearance, and the streets are arranged rectangularly, like the upper part of New York. In fact, much of Christiania recalls older parts of New York to any one acquainted with both cities.

Christiania lays no claim to being one of the first capitals in Europe, either in importance or in population, the inhabitants numbering only one hundred and twenty thousand. But few can compare with it in situation. It stands on the Akers-Elv, at the base of the Egeberg, at the head of the beautiful Christiania Fjord. While Norway can rival the view elsewhere, and even in some districts surpass it, yet the sail up the fjord on a fine summer's day is long remembered by the traveller, the more so if the North Sea has proved but a restless and trying pathway to its sheltered and stiller waters. The scenery is less grand and imposing than that afforded by the great fjords on the west and north-west coasts, but the numerous islands, the many little hamlets and villages, the variety of rocky islets and well-wooded districts, make Christiania a charming portal to Norway.

There is not much in the city itself to detain any but a leisurely traveller, but there are many scenes of great beauty in the neighbourhood. After

THE ENTRANCE TO CHRISTIANIA FJORD.

a run through the Gudbrandsdal or over the Haukelid, the luxury of the Victoria or the Royal Hotel is very welcome. The face of nature may be somewhat less attractive, but the more liberal table, and the many appliances for comfort that are found in Christiania, but wanting in the interior, render the stay there very pleasant.

The chief street is the Carl Johans Gade, a fine broad thoroughfare, extending from the railway station to the Palace. In its extent it crosses a valley of sufficient depression to make the view at either end striking. Looking from the town end, the Palace, a fine massive rectangular building, shuts in the distant view. From the terrace in front of the Palace, looking towards the east, there is a fine view over the whole length of the street and over a large part of the city, and in the distance the fjord, with the well-wooded hills that close it in. In fact, Christiania is a city of views rather than of important buildings. The fjord and the fine surrounding country afford very attractive pictures from every point of vantage. The principal shops are in the Carl Johans Gade, and in a stroll up and down this thoroughfare the wayfarer may see a good deal of Christiania and its people.

About half-way between the station and the Palace stands the large range of buildings devoted to the use of the University. This is one of the most youthful in Europe, dating only from 1811, but possessing already a considerable reputation. It bestows degrees in five faculties, possesses a large professorial staff, and has on its roll annually upwards of one thousand students. The fine collection of northern antiquities cannot compare with that at Copenhagen; still, to those who can give a little time, it can impart much valuable and interesting information about ancient Norway. The University also possesses a museum containing botanical, ethnographical, and other collections.

To the great majority of English visitors the chief place of pilgrimage in the University is the shed in the rear of the block of buildings, where now is kept the Viking's ship. The building containing this treasure is a very commonplace wooden erection, but the object itself is of priceless value, not only to the antiquarian, but to all who are interested in the early history of England. For in ships exactly like this the bold Vikings crossed the North Sea and sailed up the English rivers. Out of vessels like this they poured forth to the battle of Hengestdun, to the siege of London, to the harrying of East and West Anglia, to the sanguinary conflicts that at last placed the crown of England upon the brow of Cnut.

Artists and antiquarians have in the past exercised much ingenuity and imagination in attempting to depict accurately these vessels. The discovery of this ship has brought upon their efforts a humiliation that is softened only by the knowledge that the true sea-rovers' craft is a finer vessel than they had conceived it possible for the shipbuilders of eight hundred years ago to produce.

The discovery was accidentally made in 1880 at Gokstad, in the neighbourhood of Sandefjord. When a Viking died, his body was sometimes placed on his vessel, the sail was spread, the ship was set on fire, and the old sea-rover ended his career on the element he loved so well. But at other times the body was laid in a sepulchral chamber built upon the deck to receive it, and then the whole buried beneath a mound of earth. It was thus that this vessel closed her career, and the blue clay of the district has preserved it through all the centuries that have passed since Ethelred the Unready fruitlessly sought by paying the Danegelt to keep possession of his kingdom.

The first impression made upon the visitor by this marvellously interesting relic is a conviction that the men who built it had little to learn from modern shipwrights. The last eight hundred years have witnessed no evolution in the art of boat-building. The lines are beautiful, the work is everywhere carefully and gracefully executed, and the best shipbuilders of modern times could not produce a craft better fitted for the work she was intended to do.

An engraving is given at page 28, which shows the vessel as she appeared when first brought to Christiania; as she probably looked when swiftly crossing the North Sea under the impulse of a favouring breeze; also the rudder, the oars, the shields, and the tilt supports, as specimens of some of the many objects of interest found in her.

Mr. Nicolaysen, the President of the Norwegian Antiquarian Society, under whose skilful supervision the excavation was conducted, has published an elaborate monograph in Danish and English, giving a full account of the vessel and its contents, and illustrated by many fine plans and lithographs. From this work we have gleaned the following interesting facts.

Near the little town of Sandefjord, in the district of Jarlsberg, at the entrance of Christiania Fjord, stands the little hamlet of Gokstad. This place consists of a few farms dotted over a plain, and for centuries past the successive generations of inhabitants have known of the existence hard by of a tumulus called, as most such spots are, the King's Mound. It stands about three-quarters of a mile from the head of the Midtfjord, but in full view of the sea, which in ancient times came much nearer than it does now.

In 1880 the sons on the farm hard by began to dig for the treasure which by common report the mound contained. Mr. Nicolaysen heard of this, and at length persuaded the diggers to put themselves under his guidance. The trench that was opened exposed on the second day the stem of a boat, and in a few weeks the whole ship was revealed to the wondering and admiring gaze of large numbers of visitors. It was resolved to remove it for better preservation to Christiania, a feat causing a good deal of labour and anxiety, but at length successfully accomplished. The whole sum expended was 8700 kronor (nearly £500), of which 400 kronor were subscribed, and the rest voted by the Storthing.

The ship was somewhat weather-worn when buried, and had been built of oak, unpainted, clinker-built, and was composed of keel, stem, and stern-post, frame timbers, beams, knees, and external planking. The frame timbers were lashed to the planking by withes made from the roots of trees, and seams were caulked with a three-stranded cord made of cattle hair. She is about eighty feet long, about sixteen wide at her broadest part, and about four feet deep from gunwale to keel. She carried a mast and sail, as pictured in the engraving, but could only sail well before the wind. Hence provision was made for propelling her by oars. The bulwark is pierced on either side by sixteen holes, through which by means of a slit the long oars could be thrust outwards from within. When not used each opening was closed by a shutter, to prevent the sea from washing in.

The steering was done by a rudder fastened to the starboard side of the stern, some few feet forward of the stern-post. This was secured to the vessel by a rope, and was moved by a tiller. The steersman sat or stood facing the prow, and when the ship's course was to be starboard drew the rudder towards him, and thrust it outwards when desirous of going in the opposite direction.

The vessel contained thirty-two shields, which were suspended as represented in the engraving. They are made of pine-wood, and originally had a metal rim and centre boss, and, though of but slight avail against the direct force of a Norse axe, doubtless often served to turn blows that might have proved dangerous. They were painted alternately yellow and black, and they must have presented the appearance of a set of yellow and black half-moons. The curiously carved heads, also painted yellow and black, were most probably used as ornamental supports to carry the tilt or awning which was sometimes stretched over the greater part of the deck.

She must have carried a crew of at least sixty-four men; and, counting in the Viking, steersman, and perhaps one or two others, the total reached seventy.

The sepulchral chamber took the form of a hut erected amidships. It had been, unfortunately, broken into and robbed many ages ago, probably for the sake of the weapons and jewels it contained. Its construction and object cannot better be described than in Mr. Nicolaysen's words: 'Immediately after the death of the person concerned, a spot for the future tumulus was selected, with special reference to its proximity to the sea, of which there should be a free view, so that all passers-by might see it distinctly. In the present instance, after the removal of the mould from the place chosen, the ship was drawn from the Midtfjord or from its shed to that spot, by the horses of the deceased, and there lowered, with its stem set seaward, into an excavation in the blue clay, and stayed on each side by shores. The sepulchral chamber was then erected of the timber brought thither, and the chips hewn from it allowed to remain in the ship. When the chamber was fully prepared, the corpse of the Viking, arrayed in his state attire and begirt with his arms, was drawn on a sledge, and taken through an opening left for the purpose, and placed on a couch. The opening was then closed, flakes of birch bark were placed against it, and, finally, the other articles which had belonged to the deceased were laid in the vessel, but not until many of them, the sledge especially, had been broken up. Of the animals, only the peacock, probably a favourite of the dead man, or a memento of some foreign expedition, was placed within the vessel. The horses and dogs were slain, their bodies laid close by each side of the ship, and its entire hold—the sepulchral chamber alone excepted—filled up with the blue clay, whose surface was in its turn covered with a layer of moss and hazel branches, and then the tumulus piled high over all.'

Some bones that were found in the chamber are now to be seen in the shed containing the ship. They have been carefully examined by an expert, who reported that they had belonged to a grown-up man who had certainly passed the age of fifty years, who was possessed of a very strong-built frame, but who must have been a great sufferer from rheumatism in the muscles! Perhaps this was only to be expected after the exposure of at least fifty years of wild, dangerous, Viking life. It is possibly more surprising that a Viking ever came so near the allotted age of man.

Mr. Nicolaysen finally concludes that the ship dates from about 900 A.D., that is, it may have formed part of one of Harold Fairhair's fleets, and its owner was a great chieftain who was most probably interred on the land he possessed.

Whatever other remains may yet come to light, Mr. Nicolaysen holds that 'we shall not disinter any craft which, in respect of model and workmanship, will outrival that of Gokstad. For, in the opinion of experts, this must be deemed a masterpiece of its kind, not to be surpassed by aught which the shipbuilding craft of the present age could produce.'

The chief church in Christiania is the Trefoldigheds Kirke, or Church of the Trinity. It stands well, and belongs to the Gothic order of architecture. The interior, forming a large octagon, is more impressive than the exterior. We visited it on the occasion of a grand state funeral, when the obsequies of the late Prime Minister of Norway, Frederick Stang, were held there. By the help of friends a seat was obtained among the members of the Storthing, whence could be witnessed the assembling of past and present ministers, the professors of the University, and the officials and men of high standing in Christiania. Just before the appointed hour, the King of Sweden and Norway, a fine handsome man of imposing presence, appeared, accompanied by the Crown Prince.

The coffin was placed before the altar by the side of the pulpit, and was completely hidden from view by a magnificent sarcophagus formed of beautiful flowers arranged with consummate skill and taste.

The proceedings began by singing part of an *éloge*, composed expressly for the occasion, in which the qualities and past services of the deceased were enumerated. The minister of the church then ascended the pulpit and delivered an animated and vigorous oration, lasting for about forty minutes. This we were not able to follow, but we could gather the drift sufficiently to learn that it was a *résumé* of the life and deeds of the departed. The orator was dressed in the garb of a Lutheran priest, which with its Elizabethan ruff presents a quaint appearance to an English eye, and gives the listener the notion that an old historic portrait has suddenly stepped down from its frame and thrown itself with energy into the life of the nineteenth century.

The oration over, wreaths of beautiful flowers were laid upon the exquisite flower-work which completely covered the coffin by the representatives of various learned societies and corporations. The final verse of the *éloge* was sung; the King and the Crown Prince stepped across to the mourners and expressed their sympathy with them, and then the body was borne forth, followed to the cemetery by a long procession of representative mourners. The whole scene was well calculated to interest and impress the stranger.

The oldest church in Christiania is the Akers Church. It dates back to the eleventh century, and has recently been restored. The famous evangelist Hauge is buried there: Pastor Storjohann, a name known to all Norwegian Christian workers, has sent the author the following sketch of this remarkable man :—

'In the Raadhusgade, Christiania, exactly opposite the Victoria Hotel, stands the old Town Hall, and farther up in the same street is the Hôtel d'Angleterre. With these edifices is associated in a remarkable manner the beginning and the tragical end of the life of Hans Niel Hauge, the famous Norwegian evangelist. At the close of the last century the latter edifice was a printing office. Thither came Hauge as a country lad, with his first work, *Meditations upon the Foolishness of the World*, in the hope of getting it printed. At first he was ridiculed, but opinion quickly turned in his favour when it became known that he could pay in ready money for the printing of his book. To the other building, the old Town Hall, he came seven years later, under the escort of a constable, to be imprisoned because he, a layman, had held religious gatherings.

'Between these two occurrences there lay a season of richly blessed activity. During a period of six years he had evangelised the whole country by his journeys, which were partly commercial journeys. To an astonishing extent he had filled the Norwegian dales with religious literature, which he had printed at Copenhagen, where for six months he kept three printing offices at work, and laboured himself for twenty-one hours a day, at correcting and binding the books. One of those who helped by selling the books and who carried them in a bag upon his back is said to have been crookbacked for the rest of his life.

'The country was at that time deeply sunk in spiritual darkness, and the majority of the clergy were Rationalists, from whom Hauge almost everywhere had to encounter a fierce opposition. The Danish Government, however, would scarcely have arrested his blessed revival work, by imprisoning him, had not the bishop at Bergen, where Hauge dwelt, and where every visitor to the so-called Town Hall building, opposite the Northern Star Hotel, can see his house, let an utterance escape him that Hauge had to do with much money belonging to many of his spiritual comrades, and that it was a question whether this would not be lost with him, seeing that he was not skilled in keeping accounts.

'This was, however, an absolutely groundless fear. Hauge was just as efficient in all temporal affairs as in preaching the Word of God. He was simply a universal genius. The paper-mill at Oyern, where he was apprehended, is a work of his, and has bequeathed to our times the machinery which Hauge set in motion.

'For no less than ten years, 1804 to 1814, Hauge remained in his prison, with the exception of a short interval, during which the Government took him out. At this time England was blockading the Norwegian coast, and the country was in dire need of everything, even of salt. The Government needed practical men who could prepare this from sea-water. Their thoughts then fell upon Hauge, and he was released from prison in order that he might travel round the coast and set salt-works going. When, to the great satisfaction of the Government, he had finished this task, he was compelled to go back into prison until his earthly trials came to an

THE AKERS HUS.

end in 1814. Even when the Government had denied the people the spiritual salt by means of Hauge's words, it was compelled through Hauge's instrumentality to procure for the people natural salt. But not even did this revolting treatment crush this noble, faithful witness for God, any more than did the great suffering which he had to endure, especially at the beginning of his very unhealthy prison life, which completely shattered his iron constitution.

'With the window in the second storey of the Town Hall, nearly opposite the Victoria Hotel, where Hauge used to sit, is connected a beautiful story. A friend of his had come into the town with the hope of getting a conversation with Hauge, and being consoled by him in his spiritual distress. Entrance was denied him. He stood despairingly on the opposite side of the street and gazed up at the prison window. At last Hauge looked down at him through the dirt-begrimed window. He hit upon a remarkable expedient for communicating with his disconsolate friend. He took a candle and let the wick grow so long that the light shone only with extreme faintness; thereupon he snuffed it, and the light blazed up into a clear flame. His friend went home comforted with the assurance that it was his duty to let *his* light shine!

'Visitors to Christiania are urgently recommended to pay a visit to Hauge's grave, especially as at the same time they may see the oldest church in Christiania—perhaps, indeed, in all Norway—the Akers Church, where the grave lies on the south side. An old brass pillar bears an inscription which in its every word reveals the heartfelt affection which his friends who erected the monument cherished for him. On one side of the monument stands: "Until his very last breath he remained in that faith, hope, and love which he had sought to spread abroad through Norway, by speaking and writing, by preaching, and by a pious life." And on the other side may be read: "He lived in the Lord; he died in the Lord; by Jesus' grace he enters into salvation."'

OSCAR'S HALL, CHRISTIANIA.

The Storthings Hus, or Norwegian Parliament House, an engraving of which stands at the head of Chapter I., is a prominent building situated at the corner of Akers and Carl Johans Gaden. It was completed in 1866, and contains as its chief apartments a Storthings Sal or assembly-room for the Lower House, which will accommodate 150 members and 300 of the public; and a Lagthings Sal or assembly-room for the Upper House, accommodating 40 members and 130 of the public. The annual session is held in February and March.

The Akers Hus is an old fortress, well situated near the Pipervik. The history of it is obscure, but it dates back to the fourteenth century. It is now of no military importance, but its ramparts form pleasant walks, from which fine views are obtained.

The most accessible and picturesque spot in the immediate neighbourhood of Christiania is the Oscar's Hall, with its lovely grounds. The building is a white, unpretending structure, with a conspicuous square tower, well situated on a little eminence, on the other side of an arm of the fjord, in full view of the city. It was built by Oscar I., sold by Charles XV. to the Government, but is still kept for royal use. From the large windows in the tower and from the roof, superb views of Christiania and its environs are obtained. We were fortunate enough to be in it when a thunder-cloud rolled past, emitting vivid flashes of lightning and deafening peals of thunder, and first blotting out the city from view, and then retreating off to the east, dying away into low angry mutterings, and causing the renewed view of the landscape in the fresh sunshine to appear all the more lovely and attractive from its temporary obscuration.

A curious and interesting collection of old historical relics and pictures are to be seen in the various rooms. But to most visitors the dining-room is the most attractive part of the château. It contains several striking paintings of Norwegian scenery by J. Frich, and the celebrated set of ten small paintings by Tidemand, representing the various stages of Norwegian peasant life, from infancy through youth, love, early manhood and womanhood, the cares and labours of middle life, on into the quiet rest and peace of old age. There is a richness of colouring and design, and a tenderness of suggestion about these paintings, that interest all who see them. They possess also a tender human interest, and add greatly to the attractiveness of the room. No pleasanter way of spending two or three hours can well be devised than sailing over to the Oscar's Hall, exploring the building and rambling through the grounds. A short distance from Oscar's Hall is the Hovestnen, or Hove Cottage, an old house built at Lilleherred in Thelemarken in 1738 and presented in 1883 to King Oscar by its owner, Mr. Ole Hove. It is full of antique furniture, upon which are carved many curious family inscriptions. An engraving of the interior is given at page 86.

SALMON SPEARING BY NIGHT.
(From the painting by Tidemand in Oscar's Hall.)

Another place of interest in the immediate neighbourhood of Christiania is Frognersæter, a country house belonging to Consul Hefte, a prominent man in Christiania society, and a great lover of Norwegian scenery. From the balcony a superb view in one direction of the fjord and its lovely surroundings is obtained, and in the other of the inland country.

It is time, however, to leave the capital, for most visitors to Norway prefer the country to the cities. Probably many of the loveliest nooks, the most picturesque waterfalls, and the kindliest dwellers in the sæters are never seen by the rank and file of foreign travellers; this is the good fortune of those who can leave the beaten track, and who, having at their disposal

FROGNERS.LIER.

unlimited time and possessing unlimited power of roughing it, can wander whither they will. But those who are constrained to keep to the beaten ways have the conviction that only scenes of the most transcendent beauty can surpass those which abound along the most frequented high road in Norway, the one running through the Gudbrandsdal and the Romsdal.

The railway extends to Eidsvold, on Lake Mjösen, and a long and enjoyable sail in one of the lake steamers ends at Lillehammer. To the eye as yet unaccustomed to the views of the west coast or of the Lofoten Islands, Lake Mjösen presents many interesting scenes. The character of the scenery is quiet and rural, and the hills rarely rise to any considerable height, yet the hours occupied with the sail up the lake pass easily and pleasantly. Many here become acquainted for the first time with the resources of Norwegian steamboats in providing at least as good, and often better, tables than the stations and hotels, and also to the social qualities of the ordinary Norwegian. The captain of our vessel spoke English as well as a native, partly due, no doubt, to the fact that he had spent some years, when a boy, in England. Still English is taught in all the Norwegian schools, and almost all educated Norwegians speak it fluently. They often put their fellow-passengers to shame by the kindly fluency with which they indicate in English the points of interest passed, while those whose pleasure is thus greatly increased can often utter but a few broken phrases in Norse.

The only considerable places at which the steamer calls are Hamar and Gjövik. Hamar is well situated at the head of a large bay on the east coast of the lake, having opposite to it Halgö, the only island the lake possesses. It gives the impression of being a thriving little place, and, as it is also a station on the railway from Christiania to Trondhjem, there is always a good deal of life and activity during the summer months. The town is said to date from 1152, in which year Nicholas Brakspear, the only Englishman who has ever occupied St. Peter's chair, founded here an episcopal see. Be this as it may, there certainly exist the ruins of a cathedral. Gjövik, situated on the west side of the lake, almost opposite Hamar, but at a distance of ten or fifteen miles, is a much smaller place. The views of the lake and island are very fine, and the whole district is one of the most picturesque parts of the lake.

After leaving Gjövik the steamer rapidly makes its way between the ever-contracting shores of the lake until Lillehammer is reached. From the pier the town is reached by a twenty minutes' ride up a steep winding road overlooking the lake. It is situated on the river Mesna, which rushes tumultuously along under the bridge hard by the Victoria Hotel. Many travellers spend as little time as possible here, although Lillehammer well repays the lingerer. It is a clean little place, the houses of wood looking well-built and comfortable. There are just sufficient signs of life in the way of shops to show that civilisation has not yet been left behind. Situated high up as it is above the lake, most beautiful views are obtained looking south along the water-way already travelled, and north to where the Lougen, which drains the Gudbransdal, falls into the lake.

A walk along the hilly wooded banks of the Mesna leads to a succession of very beautiful waterfalls, much more picturesque than many of the noted cascades, and yet seen by hardly one in a hundred of those who pass through Lillehammer. At one point, possessing the significant name of Helvedeshöl, or 'hell-cauldron,' the wild rush and swirl of the water over the fall and along the deep narrow ravine, through which it rushes with thunderous roar, are quite awe-inspiring. We saw them when there was a large body of water in the river, and when the gloomy depths of the falls seemed all the more impressive by their contrast with the beautiful evening sky over them and the lovely landscape around them.

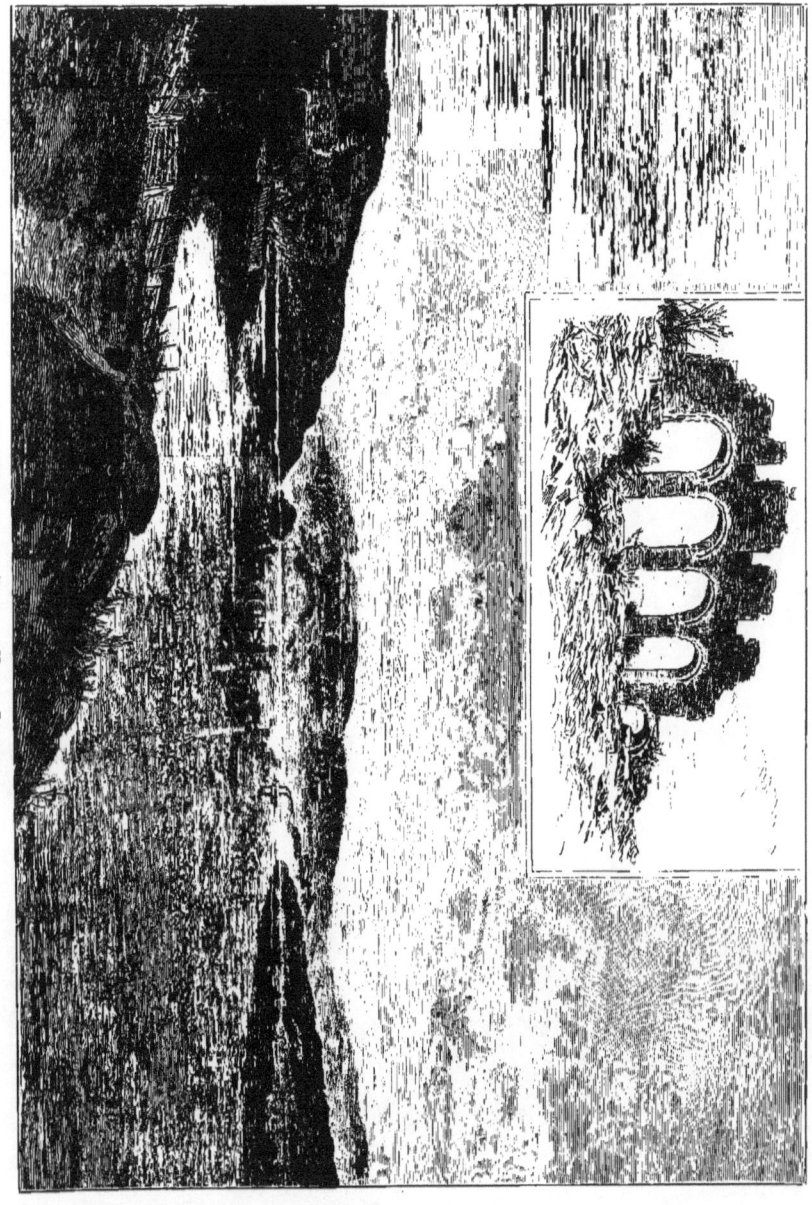

Lake Mjösen and the Ruins of Hamar Cathedral.

Lillehammer is the spot where the traveller usually makes the acquaintance of the national conveyances of Norway, the carriole, and the stolkjærre. The carriole, of which a good representation is given upon the cover of this volume, is a low two-wheeled vehicle, consisting of a framework supported upon the axle, and containing a seat for one person. Upon the end of the framework behind the rider is a ledge to which his portmanteau is strapped, and upon this sits the boy who will, if need be, drive, and who takes the pony back to the station whence it comes. Only one pony is used for each vehicle, and carrioles and ponies are kept, under Government control, along all the Norwegian high roads, and the tariff—about three-halfpence a mile— is fixed by the State. The stolkjærre, of which an engraving is given on p. 110, is a little two-wheeled cart, carrying *two* persons. Both these vehicles are more frequently without than with springs.

The roads in Norway are for the most part magnificent and kept in good repair. The ponies are wiry, active little creatures, and in the majority of instances possess the laudable desire to reach the end of their stage in the shortest possible time. The breakneck pace at which they take the descents is apt to prove trying to a nervous rider. For enjoying scenery the carriole is an admirable means of travel. There is nothing whatever to obstruct the view, and there is sufficient elevation to allow the wayfarer to see all that is to be seen.

The carriole runs easily, and long distances may be covered in a day. The writer, the first time he ever sat in a carriole or journeyed along a Norwegian highway, rode from Lillehammer to Bredevangen, a distance of 111 kilometres, or about 66 miles. And a most enjoyable day it was. He started from Lillehammer at 7 A.M., on a bright sunny June morning, and, leaving his pony very much to his own devices, was taken along a fine road at a quick trot. The town was soon left far behind, and the road began to climb higher and higher above the Lougen, which far below was speeding on to the Mjösen. Fossegaarden, the first station, is most beautifully situated high above the river, with a fine view down the valley; far below the station, and in full view of it, the river rushes over a considerable fall called the Hunnerfos.

The Gudbrandsdal is one of the most fertile and best cultivated districts of Norway. From an English point of view, the methods of cultivation are primitive, and the results scanty. The fields are small, the pastures are numerous, the farm buildings diminutive, yet the valley gives the impression that the dwellers in it are fairly well-to-do. There is certainly very little level ground, and but very few spaces where a cricket-match could be played are to be seen throughout its whole length, yet, compared with the Romsdal or Nærodal, for agricultural purposes, it is a paradise. The variety of views afforded by the river, by the lateral valleys, by the smiling fields, the tiny hamlets, the hills—first bare, and then, farther north and higher above the sea—topped with snow, is very refreshing; and most travellers will admit that there are many less enjoyable ways of spending a fine June day than by a ride up the Gudbrandsdal in a carriole.

Dinner was taken at Skjæggestad (pronounced Shěggestad), 59 kilometres, that is 35 miles, from Lillehammer, which was reached at 1.30 P.M. It is a fairly comfortable station, well situated by the high road. The landlady, like so many of the Norwegian station-keepers, seemed anxious only to make her travellers happy. A description of what happened here is typical of Norwegian station-life. Dinner began with the inevitable fish, a kind of trout, boiled; then came a rare luxury, some beef, discussed with the same knife and fork that had done duty for the fish, the landlady having hastily wiped them on a not over-clean cloth; this was followed by the famed multeberry (*i.e.* knotberry or cloudberry), a fruit resembling the raspberry, served with fine fresh cream, forming a dish that would discredit no table. The bill for the whole amounted to 1.20 kronor, equivalent to about one shilling and fivepence. The Norwegians present were also interesting and typical. At the head of the table sat an old man about seventy years of age, who could speak English with some little difficulty, and who said that he had spent a fortnight in London, in 1860. There was also at the table at Skjæggestad a sturdy farmer who had learnt English at school, and who could only speak it imperfectly, and a third whose linguistic knowledge was wholly confined to his native Norwegian. All were alike simple in manner, and kindly and courteous to the wayfaring stranger.

The next station was Listad. The sun shone brightly and the road ran near the Lougen, which every here and there widens into a lake or becomes a rapid. The valley narrows, and on either side are low mountains often white with patches of snow, and there is almost always in sight some beautiful silvery waterfall. Now and then tremendous cliffs overhang the road and look quite ready to topple over upon the traveller. At each station the proceedings were nearly identical. On alighting, the first thing was to stretch one's legs, which, when the carriole seat is low, get rather cramped; then as politely as possible to ask the first person met for *Hest med kariol* (a horse and carriole) *strax* (soon) *vær saa gud* (if you please). When the vehicle appears, it is anxiously scanned. If it has springs the ride will be fairly comfortable, if not, then a strong hope arose within that the next stretch of road might be very smooth, for the jolting in a springless carriole is somewhat considerable. The portmanteau is strapped on behind, the *skydsgut* (pronounced shysgoot)—who is in theory always a boy, but in practice is often a boy, sometimes a full-grown man or a woman, and not unfrequently a little girl—mounts upon it; and away we go, at first slowly, and then as quickly as the pony can trot.

At Listad the man who put in the pony said something which, after reflection, was interpreted to mean that the *skydsgut* was already at the next station. So off I went alone, driving along an unknown road in a foreign land, and able to carry on but a very limited conversation with any native who might have either the desire or right to hold any intercourse with the traveller. The pony was very strong and active, the carriole *without* springs, the road fortunately smooth and often down-hill, and that stage, twelve

VIEW IN THE ROMSDAL, SHOWING A NORWEGIAN ROAD.

(*From a photograph by Mr. G. H. Hodges*)

kilometres—five and a half miles—long, was completed in about thirty-five minutes.

Bredevangen was reached about 7 P.M. The last stage was somewhat trying. The atmosphere had become bitterly cold, partly because evening was advancing, and partly because the road ran at a level high above the sea. The stage was one of the longest in the day's journey, 16 kilometres. The pony was sturdy and willing, but the carriole springless, and the road, having been recently mended, was very rough and stony. Wearied and jolted, the sight of the station was hailed with gladness, and my *skydsgut* was paid off at once. He was a small boy, and, like many of his class, had exhibited a staidness and a gravity far beyond his years. He was not clean, and he came up and soberly held out his hand to shake mine. I responded, and then entered the inn, feeling that at any rate the last fee of the day had been satisfactory to the recipient. This custom of hand-shaking is one which, it may be feared, will soon disappear before the tourist civilisation from which Norway seems likely to suffer severely; if so, it will be matter for regret. The custom is one of many proofs that the Norwegians are kindly and simple in their relations with each other.

Bredevangen is a tiny hamlet, prettily situated at a junction of valleys; hills on all sides of it, a lake in front, and on the opposite hillside a cascade, like a silver streak, falling gracefully down for a thousand feet. The attendance was good, and things were neat and clean. The beds were absurdly short, but the rooms were good and the food abundant. The waiting was done by the station-keeper's wife and sister in the picturesque Gudbrandsdal costume. The bill tendered when leaving is a curiosity, forming a contrast indeed to many hotel bills that, by their exorbitant charges, have done much to banish previous good impressions of a foreign town. The three meals of the day in Norway are always substantial. At Bredevangen at *frokost* (breakfast), *middag* (dinner), and *aften* (supper), there were at least two hot dishes. For two nights' lodging and five *substantial* meals the bill amounted to seven kronor—that is, seven and tenpence-halfpenny!

Beyond Laurgaard the Pass of Rusten is reached, one of the wildest and finest scenes out of the Romsdal. The river has forced a way through a precipitous ravine, and the road winding along the side leads down a chasm that grows ever wilder and wilder until a bridge is crossed at the bottom, from which a very fine view is obtained. The scenery after this point becomes more bleak, and the road gradually ascends until Dombaas is reached. This station stands at the union of the roads from Veblungsnæs and Trondhjem respectively. It is consequently busier, larger, and more expensive than most. The traveller touches civilisation again here by means of the telegraph. It stands at an elevation of over 2000 feet above the sea, and even in June possesses a keen bracing atmosphere, not unfrequently bitterly cold. The road beyond traverses a fine upland valley, affording good panoramic views of snow-covered mountains and fir forests. The river widens out at last into the Lesjeskogen Vand, a series of three lakes about 2070 feet above the sea, from which on the east the Lougen flows down into Lake Mjösen, and thence to Christiania Fjord, and on the west the Rauma into the Molde Fjord. From Holsaet those who are fond of mountain scrambling and botanising can get abundant amusement. Hugh Macmillan, in his *Holidays in High Latitudes*, describing an ascent of one of the Dovrefjeld mountains, about 4000 feet high, gives a very interesting account of the botanical treasures to be met with, not only in that but in many other parts of

THE SLETTAFOS.

Norway. 'The season of my visit,' he writes, 'happened to be a late one. Few of the Alpine plants had yet begun to flower; but in many places exposed to the sun I observed enormous patches in full bloom of the Alpine azalea. The foliage could not be seen for the multitude of rosy flowers. Its beauty was greatly enhanced by a setting of reindeer lichen, which

THE TROLLTINDERNE.

whitened the ground everywhere with its snow-white, coral-like tufts. The rosy flowers of the azalea gleaming among these lichens, looked like rubies or garnets set round with filagree work of frosted silver or carved ivory. Every dry stony knot was covered with the compact, cushion-like masses of the Greenland saxifrage, with dense tufts of the Alpine *Lychnis*, or with carpets of campion. Here and there, in marshy places, the rare *Andromeda hypnoides* formed bright green mossy tufts, from whence arose a profusion of slender, hair-like, crimson stalks, each bearing a single white bell-shaped blossom. Side by side with it grew the *Pedicularis lapponica*, whose soft yellow blossoms formed a pleasing contrast; and the globular, snow-white heads of the rare cotton-grass. But it was amongst cryptogamic plants that I gathered the richest harvest. On this Norwegian plateau we have the exact counterparts of the *tundra*, or plains that border the Polar Sea, covered almost exclusively with dense masses of the same crytogamic vegetation, and forming the pastures of innumerable reindeer.'

A few miles beyond Mölmen the grandest part of this highway begins, the far-famed valley of the Rauma. After spending a night at Mölmen, on starting early next morning in the middle of June, the writer found that a snow-storm, which had been severe even in the valleys, had covered all the mountain-tops with a robe of exquisite whiteness. The road lay over a level valley, and the mountains close it in like a wall. In the brilliant morning sun the sharp peaks shone like gigantic diamonds, and the rounded tops were gloriously white with a purity to which no earthly art could attain. It was

THE ROMSDAL HORN.

a morning hour never to be forgotten and was a fit prelude to a day of unimagined enjoyment. 'Thy righteousness is like the great mountains,' sang the Psalmist; and, looking upon the everlasting hills robed in their spotless dress, the mind received an impression, never to be effaced, of the Divine omnipotence and the Divine purity. On nearer approach the landscape gained in impressiveness and beauty, the separate peaks stood out more boldly, and view after view opened out of ridges and hills stretching away in all directions, and each exhibiting a different intensity of whiteness. All equally pure, and yet each so tempered to the eye by its angle of reflection as to preserve an individuality that could be perceived though not expressed in words.

At Stueflaaten, the next station, the Romsdal proper begins, and it at once captivates and awes the traveller. The road winds in a zig-zag down the side of the huge ravine through which the Rauma thunders in a succession of falls, cataracts, and rapids. The gloomy depths of the gorge, the roar of the river, often hidden from sight, the grassy wooded slopes of the hills, and the bare, jagged, snow-capped mountains, combine to delight the eye and to solemnise the thought of the wayfarer.

Before reaching Ormeim, the station next in order, the carriole stops, and a walk of a minute or two brings into view the Slettafos, one of the most fascinating of the host of impressive waterfalls abounding in this region. Although the bridge, which is placed almost directly over the fall, is strong and stoutly built, yet the water rushes beneath with a velocity and a roar that renders it somewhat trying to look down upon the foaming waters as they dash on their way down into the valley.

Ormeim is famed for its fine view of the Vermedalsfos, a cascade nearly a thousand feet high that falls in three separate streams down the opposite bank of the Rauma. Beyond Ormeim the valley opens out into a broad level expanse, with the river winding smoothly and peacefully through it, shut in by lofty mountain peaks.

The road bends in and out among huge boulders and masses of rock that have been brought down in mighty avalanches from the cliffs above. Wherever the eye turns it rests upon waterfalls coming sheer down 1000 or 2000 feet from the almost perpendicular mountains. The most noted at this part of the Romsdal is the Mongefos. Mr. Mattieu Williams, in his *Through Norway with a Knapsack*, gives a description of this fall that *cæteris paribus* applies to many others in this wonderful land. 'Looking up,' he says, 'with an effort that strains the neck, to the frowning wall of rock, a torrent is seen, pouring apparently out of the blue ether. It bends smoothly over the topmost edge, as blue as the ether itself, lustrous and crystalline with the light that shines clear through it; then it is lost, having made a first plunge of a hundred feet or so down into a boiling cauldron, which it has pounded out of the rock by its everlasting thumps; but again it reappears, shattered to snowy fragments, and, striking the rock once more, spreads out and tears down a long rugged slope in white fleeces of broken water. At every resisting ledge clouds of fine spray and mist are dashed forth, the sunlight tinting them here and there with bands of the glorious iris. Then a great ledge bars its path, and it bounds upwards and forwards into the free air; and, thus bruised and battered to mere water-dust, so fine and light that it struggles even with the slight resistance of the air, it descends with slow, unvarying speed some four or five hundred feet more; then it showers upon another slope of rock, spreads into a multitude of little rills, and disappears again, till at last it rushes under the road to join the Rauma, and keep its company to the all-absorbing sea.'

After leaving Horgheim the climax is reached, and the engraving which stands as frontispiece to this work may convey some faint notion of the grandeur of the scene. The height of the mountains and the purity of the atmosphere combine to deceive the traveller. Mile after mile is traversed, until he reaches a narrower part of the valley, which bears abundant traces of mighty natural convulsions in the past, and sees the weird fantastic cliffs of the Trolltinderne, or witch-pinnacles, on the left, and, towering up over five thousand feet above him on the right, the finely-proportioned Romsdal Horn.

The Trolltinderne are perhaps the most weird and wonderful rock-masses in Norway. They seem the fit abode of trolls and other uncanny beings. Inaccessible, jagged and forbidding, they present many faces, according to the atmospheric conditions under which they are seen. Even under the bright June sunshine they were anything but inviting, and when half hidden in mist, or when dimly outlined under the moonlight, the eerie feeling they impart to the beholder would be greatly intensified. The legend runs that the succession of jagged peaks represents a wedding procession on the road to church: the fiddler, the best man, the priest; and then two peaks, struggling as it were to avoid each other, stand for the bride and bridegroom, who have most unwisely quarrelled. They are followed by the father and mother; and, last of all, a mass of rock with some resemblance to a figure stands for the lover about whom the quarrel has occurred, and who is making a last desperate effort to release the bride from a match she detests. At this critical moment they were all turned to stone, and have so continued.

The Romsdal Horn rises sheer up from the valley to a height of 5090 feet. From its peculiar pointed shape it appears to dominate the whole district, although it is not actually the highest mountain. It was long considered inaccessible, and the opinion prevailed that it had never been ascended. But of recent years it has been scaled on several occasions, and a cairn was discovered on the top that seems to have been erected there in 1827.

The best way to enjoy this grand gorge is to approach it from the Gudbrandsdal. The quiet scenery of that valley is a good preparation for the wild and tremendous views of the Romsdal. From Stueflaaten onwards at every mile the stern impressiveness increases. For the last few miles on either hand are awful precipices. To the nervous eye the mighty overhanging masses of rock seem to be preparing for instant descent upon the traveller, and the utter weakness of man in the face of the mighty forces is borne in upon the thought. And yet, seen in the bright sunlight of a June afternoon, few regions on earth can be as attractive as the northern end of the Romsdal. The wilder and sterner scenes of nature attract and repel the mind at the same time, but the sensation is one of curious fascination. And in this noted valley, for mile after mile, at every turn, huge cliffs, curiously shaped mountain peaks, sheer precipices, and waterfalls great and small, alternately delight and repel the eye, which cannot, in either case, refrain from gazing more and more intently upon scenes so unlike anything ever beheld before.

After passing the Romsdal Horn, the valley widens out, and at length Veblungsnæs is reached. A lovely sail of a few hours along the beautiful Molde Fjord brings the traveller either to Vestnæs or Molde. Every mile or so affords some new view of the numerous mountains, and, though the Romsdal is fast left behind, for hour after hour the eye dwells fondly upon its towering peaks.

THE STOLKJÆRRE

THE WEST COAST AND FJORDS.

THE NÆRODAL.

A SALMON NET AND STAGE.

CHAPTER V.

THE WEST COAST AND FJORDS.

CHRISTIANSUND—MOLDE—MOLDOEN—HORNELEN—THE GEIRANGER FJORD—THE NORD FJORD—BERGEN—
THE HARDANGER FJORD—ODDE—THE SKJÆGGEDALS-FOS—ULVIK—EIDE—VOSSEVANGEN—THE NÆRODAL
—THE SOGNE FJORD—LÆRDALSÖREN—BORGUND CHURCH—OVER THE FILLEFJELD.

MUCH of Norway's grandest scenery lies in the west coast region; in it are to be found many of the most enchanting fjords, such as the Geiranger, the Nord, the Sogne and Hardanger; and it possesses some of the highest mountains, largest glaciers, and loveliest lakes and valleys in the whole country. Each part of this wonderful region would require a volume to give any adequate account of the variety of natural beauty which it presents, and here it is possible to glance at only a few typical pictures.

On leaving Trondhjem Fjord in one of the coasting steamers, for hour after hour the traveller is borne past scenes like that represented in the engraving at the head of this chapter. The hills and mountains present all possible varieties of outline. In the morning they stand out sharply cut against the clear sky, clad in their robe of green and brown and gray; in the evening they are often shrouded in a beautiful bluish-purple haze. The old-fashioned *jägts*, with their great square sails, drift slowly by, carrying to Christiansund from the far north their valuable cargoes of dried fish. At irregular intervals the steamer either calls at villages or is met by the boats that bring off from the shore new passengers and carry back those who wish to land.

The first town of any importance that is reached by this route is Christiansund. The houses present from the harbour a picturesque appearance, and are built on the shores of four rocky islands. It contains about 12,000 inhabitants, and gives many signs of being an important centre of trade. The harbour is full of craft of all sizes and descriptions, the curious hilly streets are lined with shops, and the inhabitants give the impression of being more wide-awake than in most parts of the country. It is the great emporium for the *klipfisk*, or dried codfish trade. This is brought in enormous quantities from the Lofoten and other fisheries in the *jägts*, and then shipped in steamers to Spain and other parts of Europe. Some of the Christiansund merchants have, in the past, realised large fortunes, and their villas are to be seen in the most picturesque parts of Christiansund, and also in the suburbs of the yet more beautiful town of Molde. Of late years however, the trade has not been so good.

A PART OF CHRISTIANSUND HARBOUR.
(*From a sketch by Professor T. G. Bonney.*)

Molde, in fact, is the next place of note visited by the steamer, and it vies with any spot in Norway for beauty of situation, spread out as it is, along the foot and up the lower slopes of a high hill on the north side of a lovely fjord. The calm clear waters stretch away for miles to the east and to the west. Sheltered by the hill that rises abruptly over it and protects it from the north, Molde is one of the flower-gardens of the land. Roses, honeysuckle, and other flowers not frequently met with in other parts, flourish here, and the little town lies embowered in groves of fruit-trees, limes, birches, and pines. From the Moldehei, the sheltering hill, over 1300 feet high, one of the most extensive and satisfying landscapes delights the eye. The journey through the Romsdal valley usually terminates at Molde, and from the top of the Moldehei a last long lingering look can be given to the huge mountain masses of that district. The eye ranges over the white wooden houses of the town, over the peaceful fjord dotted with islands and enlivened by boats and steamers, over the nearer hills and more distant fjords stretching away to the south, and then rests with delight upon the tremendous wall of snow-covered peaks which shut in the distant view. Seen as the writer saw them, covered with virgin snow, gleaming dazzlingly white in the morning sun, and forming a bold contrast with the dark precipices, too steep for even a snowflake to find lodgment, they present a picture no less impressive than when slowly riding under the fantastic pinnacles of the Trolltinderne or rounding the mighty base of the Romsdal Horn.

Four or five hours' sail to the south of Molde is Aalesund, another busy, prosperous little town, much occupied with the cod-fishery.

The coast southwards from Aalesund possesses the same general features: islands in the foreground, mountains over-topped by glaciers in the distance. A few miles north of the entrance to the Nord Fjord the little land-locked harbour of Moldoen is reached. The entrance is through one narrow and winding strait, and the exit by another; and when the steamer is lying waiting for the boat from the shore, she seems to be resting on the still waters of a lovely lake. On all sides are boldly outlined hills. The houses in the little hamlet seem more neat and picturesque than they would probably appear on a closer acquaintance. As soon as the vessel heaves-to there is a bustle and stir at the little landing-stage.

A DECK PASSENGER.
(*From a sketch by Professor T. G. Bonney.*)

The water is too shallow for the steamer to come in shore, so speedily a boat like that shown in the engraving on the next page puts out from the land. It is wide, flat-bottomed and roomy. In the centre the luggage and freight are piled up, not unfrequently a cow or two find a place; at either end, and upon the boxes and bales, the intending passengers sit or stand. The stranger will often witness, in watching over the side the unloading and loading of these shore-boats, many interesting illustrations of Norwegian peasant life, and many exhibitions, sometimes amusing, sometimes pathetic, of our common humanity. The studies from life during a coasting voyage in Norway are often quite as novel and invigorating to the jaded tourist as the studies from nature.

The coast between Trondhjem and Bergen is sometimes described as tame and monotonous, and certainly the enjoyment it affords will depend to a large extent upon the temperament and likings of the traveller. But with regard to one part of the route, a little south of Moldoen, there can be no question. It is not too much to say that the voyage is well worth taking, simply to sail through the Skate Sund, and around the mighty cliff Hornelen. Soon after leaving Moldoen the steamer crosses the mouth of the Nord Fjord. This, like the entrance to the Sogne Fjord farther south, gives no hint of the superb scenery afforded along its inner reaches. The mountains are low, rocky and bare, and look as if they had been ground down by some mighty glacier action in a remote age. Suddenly the steamer enters a

THE BOAT COMING OFF TO THE STEAMER.
(*From a sketch by Professor T. G. Bonney.*)

narrow and beautiful sund, and gradually draws near to the enormous rocky mass of which an engraving is given on page 38. At one point the cliff, towering up for 3000 feet, seems to quite overhang the steamer, and, on the whistle being blown, a whole series of splendid echoes is started, the sound being tossed in succession from one part of the over-hanging cliff to another. Looking upwards from the deck to the frowning cliffs so high above it, an impression of man's insignificance is obtained similar to that felt when driving slowly along the base of the Romsdal mountains. The stupendous mass of rock juts out into the Sund, forming a bold promontory, which is slowly rounded by the steamer; and, as it begins to pass into the distance, it appears to possess the form of a gigantic fortress, with huge buttresses and a superb tower. Looking upon it, one feels how appropriate it is that it should have become associated with Norway's typical hero, the brave and splendid Olaf Tryggveson. Mythical though the story doubtless is, yet there is a certain fitness in reading how, when one of his men had scaled the inaccessible peak, and

A View in the Geiranger.

then, his nerve failing, was unable to descend, the king went to his rescue, and brought him safely down.

The steamboat journey from Aalesund to Bergen is pleasant and unaccompanied with fatigue. There are, it is true, many scenes of beauty and even grandeur on the route, but the most varied and imposing scenery lies along the overland route. Those who wish to travel this way must be prepared to rough it a little and to spend at least three or four days more *en route*, but those who can make the effort have their reward.

For most travellers the chief interest attaching to Aalesund is the fact that from it the steamer starts for the Geiranger Fjord, which, in the opinion of Norwegians, contends for the palm of beauty and impressiveness with both the Næro and Jorund Fjords. The whole district is remarkable for wild and grand scenery, culminating in the Geiranger. This fjord is about twelve miles long, and is in many parts a narrow stretch of water with cliffs towering up almost perpendicularly from 1800 to 4000 feet above the level of the sea. On either side are numerous waterfalls, one of them, known as the Seven Sisters Fall, being exceptionally graceful and beautiful. Seen either from the deck of the small steamer, or studied more leisurely while being rowed up to Meraak, at the head of the fjord, the stupendous cliffs, the traces of mighty avalanches, the strangely outlined rocks, and the countless waterfalls, all tend to convince even the sceptical that the Geiranger rises to the level of encomiums which, when first heard, seem extravagant.

THE SEVEN SISTERS FALL.
(*From a photograph by Mr. G. H. Hodges.*)

The falls in several parts of this fjord descend sometimes 2000 to 3000 feet, and exhibit in its most novel form one characteristic of these lofty cascades, viz.: the slowness with which the water descends and the gauze-like appearance it presents. This is due partly to an optical illusion, since the cliffs and mountains are on so large a scale that the distance travelled seems much less than it is. But it is also actual, as the water in falling becomes broken up in a kind of mist to which the

THE HORNINGDALSKOKKEN.

air offers greater resistance. High up on the sky-line here and there are seen little patches of arable land, and on them in what from below seem very dangerous situations, are little farms. The goats and the cows are carefully tethered, lest they should fall off to their swift destruction, and the children that are born in these cloudland farms, when out of doors are also made fast to stakes until they acquire the knowledge that it is dangerous to go too near the edge of such precipices as those upon which they are perched. If any one dies there in winter, the funeral has to be postponed until the summer, when only is it possible to carry the body down the precipitous pathway and take it by boat to the often far-distant churchyard.

On leaving the Geiranger Fjord the steamer touches at Hellesylt, a village at the end of the Sunelvfjord, the starting-point for the ride to Bergen. The view down the fjord is one of great beauty. A few miles from Hellesylt is the station of Kjelstadli, remarkable only for the fact that from it an easy excursion can be made to one of the most extraordinary mountains in the country, the Horningdalsrokken. The altitude of this peak, it has been said, corresponds well with the length of its name. It pierces the clouds to a height of 5010 feet, and from a distance presents the appearance of an unscaleable pinnacle of rock. It also forms a notable object in the famous view from the top of the road between Utviken and Red. The engraving opposite will give a better notion of its strange form than any description. The name means the Horningdal 'distaff.'

The Nord Fjord is touched at Faleide, a noted station on the Invik Fjord, one of its innermost branches. The glimpse we are able to give of it will help to recall its beauties to those who have seen them, and may convey some faint impression of their character to those for whom a visit is a pleasure still in store. But it must ever be borne in mind that no description and no engraving can impart any adequate impression of the wonderful clearness of the Norwegian atmosphere, and the marvellous beauty of colouring exhibited in the landscapes.

From Faleide to Utvik the passage is made by steamer, or, when that is unavailable, by row-boat. Of all varieties of Norwegian travel, the latter is perhaps the most enjoyable to the true lover of nature. The pleasure of course depends to a large extent upon the weather, and the character of the rowers. But, given fine weather and civil, kindly boatmen—the kind usually met with—and no hours can be more full of keen and intense enjoyment than those spent in a long row along the Geiranger Fjord, or the Ringedals Vand, or the Bredheims Vand. One seems much more alone with nature than on the deck of even a small steamer; the cliffs seem mightier, the voices of mountain and lake more audible, the inward thoughts more deeply stirred. The hours spent thus on lake or fjord are likely to linger long in the memory.

Landing at Utvik, the journey is continued by stolkjærre to Red. The vehicle is needed mainly to carry the baggage. The road climbs up a hill over 2000 feet high, and most prefer to walk. From the top a very fine view is obtained over the Invik Fjord, the Bredheims Vand, the spurs of the great Jostedalsbræ, and the surrounding mountain.

VIEW FROM FALEIDE.

By way of Förde the road runs on to the Jolstervand, a lake fourteen miles long, and at the western end the station of Nedre Vasenden is reached. The engraving represents part of the out-buildings of a farm belonging to this place. It illustrates the custom of building a number of small houses rather than one or two large ones, the idea being that if one catches fire, the others may escape; and also the way in which buildings are clustered around the cataracts.

From the Jolstervand, the road runs by Förde to Vadheim, where the steamer for Bergen is met. Of this, as of most parts of Norway touched upon in this volume, we have been able to give only a very slight sketch. The region is less explored than most parts probably because it is more difficult of access and

FARM AT NEDRE VASENDEN.

the accommodation is not so good as on the more frequented routes. Yet for fjord, glacier, mountain, and lake scenery it can more than hold its own, and compensates for the labour involved in a visit by the comparative scarcity of the ordinary tourist. If the beaten track is left, the bold traveller will have the country very largely to himself.

A little north of the entrance to the Nord Fjord is the notorious Stadt headland, one of the few points on the coast exposed to the full force of the Atlantic, and not unfrequently those who skirt it find the ocean in a troubled mood. We found the sea as quiet as we could wish, but a little south of the headland we ran into that most dismal of sea afflictions, a fog. We slowly felt our way for some hours, and then suddenly went ahead at

BERGEN.

full speed. We found on inquiry that we were sailing by time. An open space had been reached and we were to sail forty-five minutes. We did so, and in five minutes after the engines stopped found the narrow entrance aimed at, though the fog was dense enough to make all objects indistinct at a distance of fifty yards. Next to the coast itself the most wonderful thing in Norway is the skill with which the pilots manage the steamers.

Delay was fatal to our plans. We were to meet friends from England, who would be dismayed if we were not on Bergen Quay when the Domino arrived. Our fears were not groundless since the steamer following ours was detained two whole days. But we crept slowly on, and at length reached Bergen only a few hours late.

Midnight in a time of fog is not the best season for making the acquaintance of a town noted for the beauty of its approaches and sur-

BERGEN HARBOUR.

roundings. But the Ole Bull, the steamer that brought the writer from Trondhjem, had been compelled by stress of weather to reach Bergen under these circumstances. It was by no means dark, and the boatmen were as eager to carry us across the harbour to the Torvet landing as though it had been midday. It was a curious scene. The town, for the most part, was asleep. We rowed past antique wooden warehouses, dimly looming through the mist, past huge steamers of the most modern construction, on which not a light could be seen, past the curious-looking *jägts* laden most unmistakably with fish, until we reached the head of the harbour; and in a few minutes were walking up the broad Torvet or market-place.

In the glory of a superb July morning, which succeeded a day and a night of fog, the writer was able to appreciate the great natural beauties of Bergen. It is a large town of about 40,000 inhabitants, rich in historical associations, and wealthy as a great centre of commerce. Bergen is built around a harbour called the Vaag, and with its wooden houses and their bright red roofs, with its wide market-place, with its Walkendorff Tower and many churches, presents a most attractive picture. The best point of view is a magnificent road called the Drammens-Vei, built along the slopes of the grand hill, the Flöifjeld, that shuts in the town on the north and east. Standing on this road to the right, the old part of Bergen is seen, the Tydskebrygge, where the steamers lie, the Walkendorff Tower, dating from the thirteenth century, and the quaint German-looking houses that stand still as memorials of the wealth and influence of the Hanseatic League. To the left is the cemetery, the lepers' hospital, and the suburb containing the beautiful houses and gardens of the wealthy merchants. Across the harbour is the peninsula on which stand most of the modern buildings, the Strandgade with its fine shops and crowded warehouses, the Custom-house and other public buildings. And encircling the town, and closing in on every side the view, stand the hills which, to the eye of the uninitiated, appear to be only four in number, but which the patriotic dweller in Bergen asserts to be, even as those on which the Eternal City is built, in number seven. Be this as it may—whether the visitor gazes out from a pleasant window, or stands at the fish-market near the head of the harbour, or walks along Drammens-Vei, or climbs the distant slopes of one of the guardian hills that stand around her, Bergen everywhere presents pictures that strangely blend the ancient and modern, commerce and nature; the eye resting at one moment on the everlasting hills, at another on scenes of barter; at one moment on the latest product of a Clyde iron-steamship building-yard, at another on a vessel that shows exactly the same lines as those exhibited by Norse vessels before the Battle of Hastings had been fought.

Fine weather is essential, if all these things are to be seen to advantage. Yet it is certain that the chances are against this, for Bergen is noted as one of the rainiest spots in Norway. Great is the store of umbrellas it possesses, and brisk is the trade in waterproofs; but greater still is the trade in fish. Enormous quantities of dried cod, cod-liver oil, and pickled herring are sent forth every year, mainly to the Roman Catholic countries of Europe. Bergen is also the great centre of trade for imports to supply the west and north of Norway. There were many fine shops, such as Brandt's, where Regent Street prices may be paid for Norwegian furs, and Hammer's, where the same may be given for Norwegian silver.

The inhabitants of Bergen are less stolid and more given to outward signs of cheerfulness than dwellers in other parts of Norway. There is much life in the streets; the faces are bright and intelligent, and education is very carefully looked after. An amusing proof, not only that English is taught in the schools, but that the children are able to display their learning, came under the writer's notice. Walking along the street, I saw a bright girl about ten years old smiling at me, and seemingly wrestling with some thought too great for utterance. But at length she said, 'What o'clock is it?' I promptly gave her the required information, and she went on her

A NORWEGIAN HOUSE OF THE BETTER CLASS.

way rejoicing to know that her sufferings in school had not been in vain, for she had been able to converse with a live Englishman.

Du Chaillu, in his *Land of the Midnight Sun*, has noted the evidence furnished by Bergen to the excellence of Norwegian education. He writes: 'One of the pleasantest sights which strikes a stranger in Scandinavia is to see the number of children going to school; and Bergen is no exception. The whole juvenile population turns out every morning. The oldest school-building, founded in 1738, is of stone. Instruction there is free. In another part of the town is a large and more modern school, for the free instruction of boys, having a gymnasium. The upper part of the building is used for boys' and girls' classes. The school hours are from nine to twelve, and from three to five. One of the most valuable institutions is the free industrial school, where poor girls are taught the arts of female industry. It is an establishment of which Bergen may well be proud, and which every city ought to possess. The ages of the scholars range from seven to sixteen years. All work together in groups or classes, according to their proficiency—making dresses and shirts, hemming, stitching, knitting, darning —under the care of faithful and competent teachers. This school has over 500 pupils. Three hours each day are given to study, and three to lessons in the use of the needle, &c. The girls receive a fair rudimentary education, and at the same time learn how to take care of themselves and their families.'

The suburbs of Bergen, especially along King Oscar's Gade, are occupied by residences of the thriving merchants of the busy seaport. No pleasanter way of testing Norwegian hospitality or of exploring the beauties of Bergen can be imagined than that afforded by an introduction to one of these. Bergen possesses most beautiful environs, and, judging from only too brief an experience, is encircled by drives affording exquisite views, fine air, and a most enjoyable variety of scenery.

A NORWEGIAN PEASANT'S HOUSE.

The houses are built of wood, in many cases after the model of that shown in the engraving on the preceding page, and are furnished with taste and luxury. The rooms are large and well-arranged, and no homes can exhibit more perfect specimens of true courtesy and kindliness. By way of contrast, an engraving is given showing the ordinary peasant's house.

The Museum, a fine building standing on an eminence in the southern

A View on the Hardanger Fjord.
(From a painting by Carl XV.)

part of the town, is well worth a visit. The curator, to whom we had a note of introduction, was most courteous in pointing out the gems in a somewhat rich collection of Scandinavian antiquities. There is also a fine natural history collection, especially varied and complete in the birds and sea-fowl of Norway.

Bergen is the natural starting-point for the Hardanger district, and the traveller can proceed by two routes. The first is by rail, making use of the only piece of line yet constructed in Western Norway, that running from Bergen to Vossevangen. It is sixty-six miles long, and, while doubtless a great convenience, the lover of nature can but hope that the progress of railways will be slow. It abounds in tunnels, and also abounds in views of great beauty. We may be prejudiced against railways, but, even in Norway, where the rate of progression is decidedly slow when travelling by rail, you linger too long over the unattractive and far too briefly over the scenes that delight the eye and the mind.

The other route is by the steamers that ply up the Hardanger Fjord. The enjoyment of this method necessarily depends largely upon the weather. The memory of a fine day spent upon this journey will long abide as one of Norway's brightest gifts. The guide-books maintain that this route is monotonous, not to say tedious; but it is rare to find any one who has made the passage in fine weather able to speak of it in any but terms of the highest praise. The morning mist on the day referred to hung over the town, but cleared away as we started. The harbour was alive with boats rowing in to the fish market.

For the first few hours after starting the panorama of strait and island, of mountain and cloud, was a constant delight to the eye, and we found the broad Björne Fjord in a peaceful temper. After traversing this we reached a veritable fairy scene. The steamer left the broad fjord, and, turning due south, entered the entrancing Loksund. This is a very narrow strait, with cliffs on either hand rising abruptly from the water. In a small bay completely encircled by lofty hills is the tiny station of Einingevik, with only two or three houses; but, seen as we saw it, in the bright sunshine and under a cloudless sky, no description could well exaggerate the beauty of the landscape.

Sailing due south, past the island Terö, we crossed the Kvindherreds Fjord, and in so doing caught our first glimpse of the grand Folgefond glacier, covering hundreds of square miles with perpetual ice and snow. Here the Hardanger proper begins, and runs in a north-easterly direction for about fifty miles, branching out then into the Graven, Eid, and Sör Fjords. From Terö to Odde, at the extreme head of the Sör Fjord, is about seventy miles. Throughout this whole distance the fjord has an average breadth of three to four miles, occasionally contracting, especially up the branches. Like the Sogne Fjord, the Hardanger is shut in by lofty mountains 4500 to 5000 feet high; and, towering over all, visible from a thousand points of view, the vast ice masses and snow-fields of the mighty glacier. It is more visited and more popular than the Sogne, probably because so much easier of access, and supplied with stations more completely equipped for the traveller's comfort.

The slopes are more wooded, the soil more fertile, the general aspect more inviting and genial. The Sogne is severe, savage, awe-inspiring; the Hardanger a very Garden of Eden.

Every few miles the steamer stops at stations, landing cargo or taking it on board, losing and gaining passengers. Each possesses some special feature of beauty. We give a representation of one reached soon after leaving Terö, Rosendal. There is a house or two near the little pier, a few houses and a fine country mansion in the valley, and, towering aloft beyond these, the huge masses of the Melderskin, nearly 5000 feet high. Jondal, some miles further north, is most charmingly situated at the mouth of a valley, through which a little mountain stream rushes down from the exhaustless masses of snow to the fjord. The arrival of the steamer at these hamlets is the event of the day, and all within easy reach, natives and visitors, flock to the little piers. At Jondal we saw a picturesque group of the Hardanger peasantry. There had been a funeral, and a considerable company had assembled, the men in their dark clothes, the women dressed in dark petticoats, bright red bodices quaintly embroidered, with white handkerchiefs over their bosoms, and white caps, the married women conspicuous by the size of those they bore upon their heads. As the Lyderhorn swung round to pursue her journey, the moving brightly-clad

ROSENDAL.

groups seemed to give the exact amount of human element needed to complete the *coup d'œil* of a glorious landscape. Thence we passed up the lovely Norheims Fjord to Sandven, another most delightful spot, then to Utne, Eide, and finally to Odde. The afternoon and evening afforded an ever-changing succession of most lovely landscapes. As night drew on we sailed down the Sör Fjord, and at length reached Odde, almost overwhelming the genial landlord of the Hardanger Hotel with demands for accommodation.

Odde is a good centre, and those who can give the time spend several days here. Situated at the extreme end of the longest branch of the

HARDANGER PEASANTS.

Hardanger, and on the shore of the fjord, it has in front the beautiful water; behind the broad sloping valley, enclosed on either hand by mountains. Our view, showing the little station, with its wooden church, is taken from the summit of the valley, which is really a moraine, a distance of a mile and a half or two miles. On reaching the highest point, nearly 300 feet above the fjord, a beautiful lake, the Sand Vand, comes into view, which empties its waters into the Sör Fjord by the wild, rocky torrent running through the vale of Odde. Along the east shore of the lake runs a magnificent road, which leads by way of the Haukelid Pass through

Thelemarken to Christiania. From different points on the road by the lake magnificent views are obtained of the bold cliffs and mountains overhanging the west shore. It would be hard, even in Norway, to find a more inviting scene. In all directions fine views of waterfalls, mountains, lake and stream are to be had, and there is a softness about the whole region that is most

ODDE.

attractive. In the foreground of the engraving of the lake on opposite page a representation of the Norwegian method of haymaking is given.

Following the road along the east shore of Sand Vand, and passing over a road made out of detritus, a grand view is obtained of the valley through which the Buarbræ glacier descends. On the north is the Eidesnut; on the south, the Jordalsnut and the icy mass comes down to a point only 700 feet above the lake. It is an easy excursion up to the edge of the ice. Our engraving gives some idea of the scene, but the imagination has to supply the exquisite greenish-blue tints of the ice masses as seen in brilliant sunshine, the varied foliage, the variety of brown and gray tints on the sombre cliffs and mountains, and the glorious sky above, and the still bluer lake beneath. A few miles further along this road are the famous falls, the Lotefos and the Espelandsfos, the latter, when there is a good body of water coming over, among the most picturesque in all Norway, the water presenting the appearance of a veil.

The grandest natural object near Odde is the Skjæggedalsfos, (pronounced Shĕggĕdalsfos), or, as it is often called, the Ringedalsfos, by many

THE SAND VAND.

good judges considered the finest fall in Europe. It is not easy of access, and takes a full day, and necessarily the enjoyment of the traveller is greatly marred if it be either cloudy or wet. It has had the reputation of being a dangerous trip, but the Norwegian Tourist Club has done so much to improve the path that, with a good guide, ladies may venture without any hesitation. I visited it accompanied by two ladies and a guide, and, as the day was perfect—a cloudless sky and a brilliant sun—our experience was the most memorable of many memorable days in Norway.

We left Odde at 7 A.M. and rowed down the fjord to the mouth of the

Tyssaa, a stream by which the waters of the fall empty at last into the fjord. For some miles the path lies along the north bank of the ravine through which this stream flows. It is very rugged, and fit only for pedestrians, and rises and descends over masses of detritus and roots of trees. Every here

THE BUARBRÆ GLACIER.

and there it passes across huge masses of rock that have been polished perfectly smooth by the grinding force of glaciers in past ages, and which, inclined as they are at angles of twenty or thirty degrees, would be very awkward places to cross were it not for the pine-trees laid down and fastened

THE SKJEGGEDALSFOS.

so as to afford a firm foothold. A spice of danger enters in at these spots, as a lively imagination is apt to wonder what would happen if the support gave way and one began to move with accelerating velocity down one of these slopes. The impression is heightened by the sullen roar of the torrent hundreds of feet below.

The path gradually rises until it gets about 1800 feet above the level of the fjord. It takes from two and a half to four hours to reach this point, according to the walking power put forth and the resolution shown in resisting the charms of the scenery. At every hundred yards some new beauty reveals itself. You suddenly find yourself over a picturesque fall in the stream, or, looking back, you catch a magnificent view of the Folgefond glacier stretching away dazzlingly white and in glorious contrast to the blue sky as far as eye can reach.

It is true that there are times when you have no temptation to linger, but when you breathe more freely after an exciting step or two, and try to banish the thought of how you will fare on your way back. Occasionally the path runs at the very base of gigantic masses of rock that overhang to such an alarming extent that you feel as if an incautious word would bring half a mountain down upon you. The impression is heightened by seeing signs of tremendous falls that to the unaccustomed eye appear painfully recent.

At length, after about four and a half hours' hard walking, and when we were all feeling much oppressed by the glare and heat of the July sun, we reached a projecting point, and in the distance saw a beautiful little green valley with a few houses in its centre; and the guide, pointing, cried, '*Gaard Skjæggedals!*' and we knew that our half-way house was at hand. Cooling our heated faces and hands at one of the innumerable streams running down the side of the ravine, we struggled on, and soon found ourselves in the guest room of the farmhouse. There we rested and discussed the contents of our guide's knapsack, but were most refreshed by the pure cool milk which the woman of the farmhouse brought to us.

From this point the journey is mainly by boat. A very fine fall, the Mogelifos, that in any other country would be thought worth a special visit, rushes down into a small lake which is crossed in a row-boat. The little valley is shut in on all sides by hills, and is a restful, attractive spot, enjoyable enough in summer, but a dreary spot, no doubt, in the long winter. The lake ends at a cataract called the Vasendenfos, which forms the outlet of the Ringedalsvand, and which reminds one forcibly of that first wild rush with which the water from Lake Venner begins the cataracts of Trollhatta.

The Ringedalsvand is a fine mountain lake 1500 feet above the level of the sea, with water of wonderful clearness, and shut in by lofty mountains. It is about seven miles long, and the great fall is at the far end. Securing a man to assist the guide, we embarked on the smooth waters. At the western end, the foliage is rich and the hills low, but as mile after mile is passed, the scenery grows wilder and wilder. Away in the west the great Folgefond glitters in the sun, but as we draw near the end of our journey, the grim cliffs of the huge Einsætfjeld tower over us, the absence of all evidences of human life begins to grow oppressive, and nature seems to look larger and sterner and mightier than ever. At length, on rounding a projecting point, the mighty fall bursts upon our view, and we need not the guide's exclamation, 'Skæggedalsfos,' to know that the object of our quest is in view. It sends out afar the tokens of power. The surface of the lake is troubled by the rush of the water, and while fully half a mile away the spray, borne on the breeze, dashed upon our faces.

The fall is situated in an amphitheatre of rock at the extreme end of the lake. The bare black cliffs that encircle it present a most forbidding aspect, and one feels as though the sight of a dragon or giant bearing off a lovely maiden, or of enchanted castle, would be in perfect harmony with the weird surroundings.

We landed, and climbed up to a point of rock whence a good view of the fall is obtained. An enormous mass of water comes over the cliff in a perpendicular fall of about 530 feet, and beyond it are several smaller falls. The forms the water assumes in its descent are very beautiful. It strikes the foot of the cliff with a thunderous roar, dashes madly along for a hundred yards or so, and then in a furious cataract, penned in between mighty rocks, rushes down into the lake.

THE TYSSESTRANGENE.

The height of the fall, and the enormous mass of water that rushes down the face of the cliff, are very impressive. But the most striking evidence of power is given by the rushing tempest that the fall creates. It is possible to reach a rocky projection near the base of the falling water; but it is difficult to remain there with any comfort. A violent wind sweeps down, bringing with it drenching clouds of spray; the thunderous roar drowns all efforts at conversation; the gloomy surroundings awe and subdue the mind; and the curious sensation that it is dangerous to stand near the edge, and yet, drawn by an indefinable fascination, that it is needful to do so, is present in its full power. Altogether a day at the Skjæggedalsfos is a never-to-be-forgotten experience even in Norway.

THE SPRING DANCE.

As the boat is rowed back, there is time to observe the twin fall, the Tyssestrangene, situated at the head of a great cleft in the cliffs surrounding the east end of the lake. We give a representation of it on the opposite page.

At Odde we saw some peasant-dancing. The music is produced from a curious instrument of the violin class, and is not unpleasing of its kind. The dances are also characteristic and pretty to watch, the most interesting being the spring dance, of which we give an engraving.

The Hardanger district possesses, in addition to the Skjæggedalsfos, another that has long held rank as chief, the Vöringfos. To reach this from Odde, a sail by steamer down the whole length of the Sör Fjord is needful. On a bright sunny day no trip can be more beautiful. The stations are only a few miles apart, and, when we made the journey, the cattle were beginning to start for the sæters. At one little landing we saw about seventy cows standing about the pier, and were somewhat disconcerted at hearing that they were all to come on board. While we were wondering where they could possibly

K

THE VÖRINGFOS.

be stowed, a hatch was opened, disclosing a large hold beneath the main-deck. A broad band was placed under the belly of each animal, hooked on to a fall attached to the steam-crane, and in a twinkling the astonished cow was hanging in mid-air over the hatch. In far less time than I could have conceived possible, the seventy cows were transferred to the hold. One pleasant feature was the manifest affection felt by the peasant girls for their dumb friends. They patted them, spoke soothingly to them, and remonstrated with the men of the steamer when they used any needless force.

VIEW NEAR ULVIK.

The steamer, on leaving the Sör Fjord, turns into the Eid Fjord—near the eastern end is the station of Vik, the starting-point for the Vöringfos. A short walk leads to the Öifjords Vand ; an hour's row conducts the visitor to the foot of the Maabodal, and a hard two hours' walk through a wild rocky region brings him to the foot of the fall. The water comes over the cliff in

GLEN NEAR EIDE.

a perpendicular leap of 700 feet, and a dense column of spray constantly rises. In fact, it is said, and with a certain amount of truth, that the chief difference between the Skjæggedalsfos and the Vöringfos is that you can see the first, but can see only the mist of the other. The fall is best seen from below. It is only of recent years that this view has been obtainable, the Tourists' Club having made the path. Formerly it was only possible to view it from above.

Ulvik and Eide, situated, the one at the head of Ulvik Fjord, the other at the head of Graven Fjord, are the other important stopping-places on the Hardanger. Usually the steamers on their return journey call at Ulvik, and then proceed to Eide. By road over the mountains, the villages are only twelve miles apart, but by sea, as a huge promontory has to be rounded, the distance is doubled. A favourite plan is to land at Ulvik, send on baggage by boat, and then either walk or ride over the mountain ridge to Eide. The sail up the Ulvik Fjord is very fine, and the situation of the village delightful. The road soon begins to rise, and when, as in our case, the sun is shining brightly and the wind is westerly, the ascent is hot work. Yet it is one of the pleasantest walks in Norway. Snug farms are passed, fertile fields and trim little orchards lie on either side, and from successive points of vantage views of entrancing loveliness are obtained over the fjord and the surrounding mountains. The higher the road rises, the wider becomes the outlook; the farms give place to pine-forests, and at length the fjeld is reached and crossed at a height of 1200 feet above the fjord. The descent to Gravens Kirke is very steep, and for the last two or three miles the road runs along the quiet, picturesque Gravens Vand. Our journey began in brilliant sunshine, we crossed the fjeld through showers, and we entered Eide in a drenching downpour of rain, glad to reach the hospitable shelter of Mæland's Hotel, one of the cleanest and most attractive in Norway.

Eide, a little village nestled in between lofty hills at the head of the Gravens Fjord, is one of the busiest spots on the Hardanger. All the Bergen steamers call there; all travellers wishing to see the Hardanger, and who have journeyed by rail from Bergen to Vossevangen, pass through it, and those who, like ourselves, having seen the Hardanger, wish to make for the Sogne Fjord, bid farewell to the Hardanger here. It is a spot at which one would fain linger. The fjord invites to boating excursions, and gives, in the course of an hour's rowing, a succession of landscapes that can be rivalled only by other parts of the Hardanger. A beautiful little river flows through the valley from the Gravens Vand to the fjord, and opening up from the central valley are the most delightful little well-wooded glens and fairy nooks.

The road from Eide to Vossevangen is one of the most frequented in Norway, and one of the most characteristic. It passes up the course of the river, which flows with a pleasant murmur down to the fjord, and then skirts the shore of the Gravens Vand. Passing the station of Ovre Seim, it traverses the valley of Skjervet, which for impressiveness, and also as an exhibition of road-making skill, is surpassed only by the Stalheimsklev. The road soon begins to rise, and by a series of zig-zags climbs up the steep face of the mountain, until the level of the higher valley is reached. On the right hand, about half-way up, is the Skjervefos. The stream flows over black slate rock, which at the point of the fall forms a precipice of considerable height. The road, carried on arches, passes near and in full view of the fall, which presents at once a grand and beautiful appearance, the white foaming water spreading like a veil over the black forbidding perpendicular rocks. After reaching the top of the ascent, the road passes along the banks of the

Skjerselv, and then through a pine-forest, refreshing alike to the sense of sight and of smell.

By a gradual descent through a wide and well-cultivated valley, past babbling streams, diminutive saw-mills and tiny farms, we come to Vossevangen, well situated on the shore of the Vangs Vand, and noteworthy as much for its hotel accommodation as for its natural beauties. It is surrounded by one of the most fertile and well-cultivated regions in Norway, and is sometimes described as the market-garden of Bergen. The valley is broad, with the lake in the centre, and with gently sloping undulations and hills on the Vossevangen side. A row on the lake in the evening, with the sunset light on mountain and lake, is a fitting close to the day. The church is well situated, and has the advantage or disadvantage of being a place much resorted to in order to see Norwegian costumes. Many travellers hasten from Bergen on Saturday to spend the Sunday at Voss.

Vossevangen, being the terminus of the little piece of West Coast Railway, is rapidly losing the out-of-the-world charm possessed by such places as Ulvik and Odde.

We left Vossevangen at 6 A.M. on a magnificent July morning for the finest day's ride in Norway—and, with the possible exception of the Yosemite Valley, perhaps the finest in Europe or America—viz. the journey to Gudvangen. For the first few miles the road passes through well-wooded ravines, by the shores of lakes, through little groves of fir-trees, until, near the station of Tvinde, we pass the fine Tvindefos, which rushes down over ledges of rock that break up the mass of water into many different portions, and which gains a new beauty from the fact that in every crevice where a tree can find root trees are growing. After passing Tvinde, the road ascends, crosses and recrosses the Vossestrandselv, passes Vinje, and then winds for some miles along the Opheims Vand, reaching finally Stalheim, a poor little hamlet, formerly a station.

Up to this point there is nothing exceptional in the scenery. We have passed many exquisite spots—little views of the river, picturesque peeps of distant mountains, attractive bits of pine-forest, fine glimpses of lake and hill. But almost directly after passing Stalheim there bursts upon the astonished and delighted sight a scene of surpassing beauty and grandeur.

The road appears to end abruptly in a precipice, and stretching out in front is the Nærödal, a narrow valley, flanked by lofty mountains, and shut in at a distance of five or six miles by a cliff, down the face of which for 2000 feet falls, like a silver streak, the Kilefos. Immediately in front to the left rises the striking mountain known as the Jordalsnut, whose curious conical summit towers aloft to the height of 3600 feet. On the right the huge Kaldafjeld uplifts its precipitous masses to an elevation of 4265 feet. Through the valley runs a wondrously clear stream, crossed and recrossed by the road which passes along the foot of the mountains. The first impression is one of awe. The mind seems to feel that it is witnessing the result of some awful convulsion of the past ages, when this mighty cleft was made in the everlasting hills. It also experiences that curious sensation, at once attractive and repellent, the desire to go forward and explore this sombre valley, and yet the shrinking from an enterprise that seems likely to be fraught with peril.

After the first surprise has passed, and the first intensity of gazing exhausted, the question comes—How are we to reach the level of the valley? We go forward, and see one of the triumphs of Norwegian road-making. We have had frequently to note the fact that Norwegian engineers can, in the matter of road-building, hold their own with the best in the world. The Stalheimsklev or cliff is a steep, rocky slope about 1100 feet high. Down this, in no less than sixteen zig-zags, a fine broad road descends. It is easy for persons not nervous to ride down, and perhaps possible, for persons either too ill or too indolent to walk, to ride up. But the turnings are so frequent and the decline so steep that, as you lean over the rail of the topmost, you feel as if, with a little effort, you could throw a stone upon the lowest, lying a thousand feet below.

THE SIVLEFOS.

At the right-hand turn of the first zig-zag a great cleft in the mountain comes into view, and down this thunders a fine waterfall, the Stalheimsfos. At the left-hand turn of the next, the cascade pictured in our engraving, the Sevlefos, appears. Each fall alone, in other surroundings, would be considered well worth a long journey to visit. And thus the whole way down the descent, first one and then the other of these mighty cascades comes into view, delighting the eye and filling the ear. They form appropriate natural embellishments to one of the noblest engineering triumphs. By this road the descent into the valley is made, and the view looking back up the steep winding ascent and on through the narrow valley gains rather than loses in impressiveness. The mountains seem much higher, the shadows fall dark and heavy across the road, the carriage passes continually beneath enormous masses of rock that appear to need only a slight exertion of force to bring them down upon us in all their destructive might. An hour's ride, with the beetling cliffs on the one hand, and the extraordinarily clear mountain stream on the other, brings us to the door of Hansen's hospitable station, the rest and shade proving grateful to us after several hours' travelling, the last under the fierce heat of the sun at the only time when his rays can fully invade the depths of the Nærödal, viz. noon on a midsummer day.

Gudvangen, a tiny hamlet, stands at the point where the Nærödal becomes the Nærö Fjord. The land suddenly becomes water, and then the enormous mountains and precipices lift themselves up three, four, and five thousand feet above the surface of the placid waters. There is an entrancing view from Gudvangen, looking down the fjord. The best way to appreciate the natural beauties of the spot is to row along the fjord in the beautiful afternoon light; in the deepening shadows the towering cliffs become yet more impressive, and the clear-cut reflections in the water add fresh interest to the scene. In the late evening we walked up the valley and saw it under the subdued light of a July night. The stream babbles pleasantly by on its way to the fjord, sounds of near and distant waterfalls can also be heard, the road winds in and out amidst enormous boulders, and on either hand the precipitous rock walls rise up giant-like and forbidding, exerting a certain weird influence over the mind, man, in the evening stillness, seeming such an insignificant helpless atom in the presence of Nature's most impressive immensities.

At Gudvangen the traveller from Eide touches the Sogne Fjord, of which the Nærö Fjord is one of the innermost branches. The Sogne is the longest fjord in Norway, running inland a distance of 106 miles, and averaging four miles in width. It is in places 4000 feet deep. The scenery along its whole length and in its numerous arms is grand and impressive beyond any power of language adequately to describe. It needs to be seen, and once looked upon is never forgotten. It is more rugged and sombre than the Hardanger. The fjords are often narrow, and the cliffs more precipitous and less wooded. Even in the brilliant sunshine of a Norwegian summer day the Sogne exhibits Nature's frown rather than her smile. The eye is fascinated, but awed rather than pleasurably attracted.

The entrance is a little north of lat. 61°, and the steamer, after a six hours' sail from Bergen, turns eastward past the massive cliffs of the Sognefest, or Castle of the Sogne, which guards the entrance. At first the scenery

GUDVANGEN AND THE NÆRÖ FJORD.
(From a photograph by Mr. G. H. Hodges.)

is somewhat tame, the mountains low and bare and rocky. But Vadheim is soon reached, a hamlet prettily situated at the head of a little fjord of the same name.

Passing this, the vessel carries the traveller into a region that grows wilder and more imposing every hour. Stretching away on the north are the gigantic masses of the Jostedals glacier. On every hand are mountains four to six thousand feet high. Each of the great inner arms of the Sogne has its special features of interest. Those who can rough it, and who wish to see some of the vastest snow-fields and ice-caves in North Europe, journey up the Fjærlands Fjord, where also is Balholmen, a beautifully situated village, the scene of the great Frithiof's Saga.

In Tegner's version of this Saga, the following description of the region, the inheritance of Frithiof, is given :—

> Frithiof, an only descendant,
> Shared with none, and in peace he entered the homestead on Framnæs.
> Round in a circle of three miles hills, mountains and valleys extended ;
> Three sides were thus surrounded; the fourth was washed by the ocean.
> Birch-trees covered the mountain-tops, on the sunny hill-slopes
> Ripened the golden barley, and rye waved taller than giants.
> Many a lake in the fields held up to the mountains its mirror,
> Held it up also to forests, and elks with antlers prodigious,
> Wandering like kings through the wood, and drinking at murmuring fountains.
> But in far-spreading valleys, on blooming meadows were grazing
> Herds with glossy and sleek hair, udders swelling with rich milk.
> Mingled among them were numbers of sheep, and frolicsome lambs too,
> Covered with fleecy and silvery wool, resembling the heaven's
> Light and transparent clouds, chased gently by breezes of spring-time.

Most visitors to Norway explore the Sogne from either Gudvangen or Lærdalsören. The extreme eastern branch is the Aardals Fjord, at the head of which stands Aardal, the starting-point for a visit to the third great fall in Western Norway, the Vettifos. The Aardalsvand, embosomed in superb scenery, is traversed, and the valley of the Utladal leads, past Moen, to Vettifarm, near which is the great fall. The water rushes over the cliffs at the inner side of a semicircle of rocks in a perpendicular fall of 900 feet.

The Sogne scenery in its more smiling aspect is found in the Lyster Fjord, twenty-five miles long, another of the eastern branches of the main fjord. Here also is the readiest point of access to the mighty Jostedalsbræ. Its inner branches are thought to resemble the Lake Lucerne scenery. The Jostedal leads up to the glacier, which covers nearly five hundred square miles, and has the distinction of being the largest in Europe. To cross it by any of the numerous routes is, of course, a hard and fatiguing journey, to be undertaken only by good walkers and by those who are well prepared to 'rough it.'

Many who sail on the waters of the Sogne never see either the Lyster or the Aardals Fjord, but few miss the Nærö Fjord. And, in fact, to have seen the latter is not only to have looked upon the wildest, most forbidding, and most characteristic Sogne landscape, but is also to have looked upon one of the most sombre, unique districts of Europe. At Gudvangen the Nærödal glides into the Nærö Fjord. The little steamer ploughs her way through the still deep waters, only a few hundred yards wide, and lofty mountains rise up on either hand for thousands of feet, sometimes almost sheer precipices from base to summit. Soon after leaving Gudvangen, the

BORGUND CHURCH.

Bakke fall, 3000 feet in height, is seen coming down the face of the cliff. The little hamlets seem to cling precariously to the face of the rock. One feels almost overpowered by the sombre beauty and by the majesty of the scene. The fjord gradually widens out into the Aarlands Fjord, which in turn leads to the main fjord, and then a few miles' sail to the east brings the vessel to Lærdalsören.

The whole trip, which occupies several hours, is a succession of marvellous views. At one moment the boat is beneath a huge cliff that seems trembling and on the point of rushing down and for ever blocking up the narrow channel; at another she is sailing over a clear space, out of which open up a number of rocky fjords. At one time the view is limited to a few hundred yards of water, bounded on every hand by stupendous precipices; at another the eye ranges up a beautiful valley or through some depression in the fjord wall catches in the distant sunlight glorious peeps of the glacier or most lovely mountain outlines sharply defined against the clear blue sky. The colours also are most exquisite, the wonderful greens of the water, the black and purple and brown of the rocks and cliffs and mountains, the greenish-blue of the remote glacier and the serene blue of the cloudless sky—these, with their infinite blendings and combinations of tone, defy description. The eye is *not* satisfied with seeing. It would fain linger, but onward goes the vessel; one after another, hour after hour these grand and glorious visions come, and then—all too soon—the traveller finds himself at Lærdalsören, and, stepping from the boat, is besieged by carriole drivers, by boys who want to carry his luggage, by some of the convenient accompaniments of civilisation which remind him only too forcibly that he has left Nature in one of her most exalted and impressive scenes and moods, and come back to a semi-civilisation that is less attractive than ever.

From Lærdalsören a fine road leads over the Fille Fjeld to Christiania. It follows the course of the Læra, and for a few miles passes over a somewhat uninteresting plain. Beyond Blaaflaten, the first station, the route becomes full of interest. It passes over moraine deposits, and as the valley gradually narrows the scenery becomes very wild. The river has forced its way through an enormous ravine, the cliffs of which overhang the ascending road, while the river roars and thunders along eighty or a hundred feet beneath. There are many signs of the action of water on a much grander scale at some remote age.

At Husum the traveller reaches the finest part of the valley, the river foaming along in the centre, the hills towering aloft on either side. A short distance beyond Husum is situated one of Norway's marvels, the far-famed church of Borgund. It stands a short distance from the road in a broad open valley which in ancient times—before the Læra had forced its way through the tremendous ravine between Borgund and Husum—was a lake.

The first impression made by this extraordinary relic of the past upon meeting the eye of the observer is that it is unlike anything he has ever seen before. The porches, the open galleries, the numerous roofs, the curious crosses and dragons' heads, the old belfry standing hard by, combine to form a building resembled only by the somewhat similar structure at Hitterdal. It is built entirely of wood, and is believed to date back to the twelfth century. That is, it was standing before either York Minster or Salisbury Cathedral assumed their present forms. Strange also as the statement may sound, it is built upon the regular cathedral plan. Wood was used in its erection, because Norwegian builders scarcely ever employed any other material. It has escaped all the vicissitudes of seven centuries, and stands now looking probably much the same as it did before King John signed Magna Charta.

So much has been written about this building, and the visitor usually hears so much about it while on his way thither, that he is inclined to feel at first sight that it is ridiculously small. With its six tiers of roof, the highest surmounted by a small spire on which stands a cock, its curious lych-gate, and its somewhat sunken situation, it looks more like a freak on the part of the builder, or like some singular toy.

On entering, the impression of smallness is intensified, as the building is only about forty feet long and twenty wide. No services have been held in it for some time past. The Antiquarian Society watch over it with tender care as a precious possession. A new church has been put up for the parishioners, but, with a total disregard to the fitness of things, it has been placed far too near the old building.

Yet, small as the old church is, and unecclesiastical as it looks, a close scrutiny reveals the true church plan. It possesses a nave, a chancel and

BELL-TOWER, BORGUND CHURCH.

opportunities of tasting such dainties prepared by Norwegian cooks. We found, notwithstanding this, that a little reindeer went a long way.

The country about the station is very bare and drear, and the temperature, even in July, keen and cold. Snow lies on either side of the road in large patches. We spent a few moments in snow-balling, a novel occupation for a July afternoon! A visit to Nystuen convinces the wayfarer that the establishment of the station is a humane act on the part of the Government, and makes it easy to believe the stories told of the rescue of travellers very hard beset by the snow and storms of winter. Additional evidence of the same kind is furnished by the numerous snow-ploughs met with along the entire route.

A SNOW PLOUGH.

Beyond Nystuen the road descends rapidly, and beyond Skogstad Lake Vangsmjösen, 1540 feet above the sea, is reached. It is about nineteen miles long, and the road winds along its southern shore. The scenery along the whole length is magnificent, and is particularly fine at the western end. Hard by the station of Grindaheim is the mountain of the same name, 5590 feet high, and towering aloft on the northern shore is the huge Skogshorn. Beyond Grindaheim the views of the lake and mountains are very fine, and at one or two parts the road has been hewn out of the solid rock. From this point onwards the ride through the Valders district is very pleasant and beautiful, but with little of the grandeur of the west coast region. Everywhere there are signs of comfort and prosperity. There are numerous farms, some of them of considerable size. The people look peaceful and happy. The traveller at one time rides through a sweet-smelling pine forest; at another by the margin of a lake or the banks of the river; now the road climbs up a long ascent, from the top of which a beautiful view is obtained, and now for miles it steadily descends through a succession of smiling valleys.

FRYDENLUND.

Fagernæs, in the North Aurdal district, one of the pleasantest stations

L

along this high road, is beautifully situated on the shore of the Strandefjord. From the watershed to near Nystuen, the Bægna river flows down, ever and anon widening into lakes like the Vangsmjösen and the Strandefjord, the latter being seventeen miles long. The neighbourhood of Fagernæs is very lovely, and a walk through the pine forests, a visit to the neighbouring falls and streams, or a row on the beautiful lake, all tempt the visitor to hours of pure enjoyment.

A few miles from Fagernæs, lower down the valley, is Frydenlund, and from this point onwards the road runs over wooded hills—through quiet and beautiful valleys. Ever and anon the distant snow-covered mountains are seen rising up clear and beautiful above the nearer lakes and valleys, and ever and anon the road winds past prosperous farms or through groves of pine and birch trees.

Sveen, the next station, is about twelve miles distant, and the road gradually ascends, giving a succession of extensive and beautiful landscapes. Just before the top of a well-wooded plateau is reached, on looking back, one of the finest views in Norway is spread out before the eye. In the foreground is the lovely valley of Valders, with its farms and patches of woodland; in the centre is the Strandefjord, with its silvery waters; and, forming an imposing background, away in the distance are the huge snow-topped Jotunheim mountains.

After crossing the plateau, which is well covered with pine-trees, and also contains one or two swampy lakes, the road descends through fine forest country, past a large sanatorium to Sveen, and thence, beyond Tomlevolden, it ends at length in a smiling valley at Odnæs, on the Randsfjord. At Odnæs one seems to touch civilisation again. The hotel is a large one, and the travellers who have come from Christiania, *en route* for Bergen, meet there those who have crossed the Fillefjeld and are making their way to the capital. To see even thirty or forty people together appears strange after the long journey through the thinly inhabited district of Valders.

The sail down the lake, touching at the villages on the way, is a pleasant change after riding for so many days. The day was beautifully fine when we started, but we soon had experience of the suddenness with which storms arise on these lakes, and the violence also that they can exhibit. For about half an hour the sky became as black as night, it rained a deluge, and then cleared off as quickly as it came on.

The Randsfjord resembles, in its general character, Lake Mjösen, but it is smaller, being only forty-four miles long, and varying from one to two miles in width. The sail down is enjoyable, as the steamer calls every few miles at little villages, and the views along the banks are very pleasant. As the southern end of the lake is neared there are abundant signs of one of the staple trades of Norway, in the enormous number of pine-logs floating down on their way to the sea. These logs are stored in enclosures, and often many acres of water are covered by the closely-packed timber. As required they are placed in the current of the river forming the outlet of the lake, and pass down the rapids on their way to either the saw-mill or the port whence they are to be shipped to other lands.

From Randsfjord the traveller is soon carried by rail to Christiania. One of the best towns to see on the route is Hönefos. It is situated at

HÖNEFOS.

the junction of the Bægna and the Rands rivers, which form here quite a series of cataracts. Vast quantities of timber come down these falls on their way to Drammen. On either bank are sawmills, where much of the timber is cut up. The town is attractive to the traveller who can spare time, and at Glatved's Hotel he will find good accommodation in the midst of very pretty surroundings. The cataracts with their numerous sawmills are well seen from the main bridge which crosses the river, and there are walks along both banks. We saw here one of the well-known timber shoots. The vast quantities of timber that collect at the lower part of the Randsfjord are floated down the stream. Many of the logs are cut up in the Hönefos sawmills, and for those not required the shoot is prepared. It is a wooden trough running down one side of the cataract. A stream of water just large and deep enough to float the heavy logs runs constantly through the trough. The logs not wanted at the mill are guided into this trough, and then the current speedily bears them away. A bridge crosses the trough near the bottom, and it is fascinating to watch the logs descending. They are twenty to thirty feet long, and, borne onwards by the rapid current, they shoot under the observer's feet at terrific speed, plunge sullenly into the deep pool at the end of the shoot, and then drift slowly onwards along the surface of the river.

The country around Hönefos is very pretty, but, after a trip over the Fillefjeld, seems tame and comparatively uninteresting. Towns like Hönefos and Drammen exhibit many signs of business activity and prosperity; the whole district in summer is like a Garden of Eden, but it has none of the savage beauty and terrible grandeur of the west coast or the Romsdal.

A NOOK NEAR CHRISTIANIA.

SOUTHERN NORWAY.

GAUSTA.

AN OLD CHAIR IN HITTERDAL CHURCH.

CHAPTER VI.

SOUTHERN NORWAY.

CHARACTER OF COUNTRY—THE KING'S VIEW—DRAMMEN—KONGSBERG—HITTERDAL CHURCH—THE RJUKAN-FOS—FLATDAL—A THELEMARKEN FARM—WOOD-CARVING—CHRISTIANSAND—SÆTERSDAL—STAVANGER.

SOUTHERN NORWAY is the land of lakes and beautiful views. It has little in common with the unique scenery of the Lofoten Islands and the coast opposite to them, or of the Sogne and Nord Fjords. It is altogether softer and more pleasing, though less grand and stimulating, than the West and North. But it possesses, in the Sætersdal and Thelemarken, districts still untouched to any considerable extent by the influences of the great outside world. In no other part of the land are such typical men and women, such characteristic habits and customs, such curious costumes or such novel buildings, to be seen.

None visit this part of Norway without hearing enthusiastic praises of the Rjukanfos, and few leave it without attempting to visit that fall. The journey from Christiania to Kongsberg is generally made by the railway that skirts the northern shores of Christiania Fjord. From the windows of the train many exquisite views are obtained of the fjord, of hills covered with birches and pine-trees, of lovely valleys and of lakes by whose banks one would fain linger long. It runs through the very garden of Norway. A few miles from Sandviken, a station situated at the northernmost end of

Christiania Fjord, is Krokleven, a cliff that uplifts itself high above the beautiful Tyri Fjord. It is from this that the celebrated Kongens Udsigt or King's View, of which an engraving is given at page 25, is obtained.

Those who have looked out on this prospect under a clear sky and the brilliant sunshine use terms of enthusiastic delight that sound absurdly extravagant to those who have never visited Norway. And even when mist and cloud enshroud the view strange atmospheric effects sometimes reward the patient climber. Dr. Cairns, who visited the place to watch the sunrise, and on arrival found the conditions apparently most unfavourable, thus describes his experience in the *Sunday at Home* for November, 1879 :—

'I had gained my point, but, instead of sunrise, there was an obstinate mist, wrapping everything a hundred yards off in shade, and leaving the great open space, which I knew was before me, a blank firmament. The wooden stage had carved on its sides and floor the names of more fortunate visitors. Having exhausted this source of interest, I selected the most distant pines as landmarks, and began to hope that I was beginning to see beyond them. At length, about half-past nine o'clock, I felt some heavy drops of rain, and sought shelter under a clump of firs. Looking back after a minute or two, I saw something black in the sky. It was a cloud forming, and as I rushed out on the stage the mist was slowly vanishing; part of the fjords below, with the islands in them, were shining exquisitely through the seas of mist that struggled to cover them, and the distant hills in the west were gleaming forth. The only regret was that I had missed the moment of transition; but this soon gave place, for the mist again came completely over everything as before; and, in the hope that I should see the whole process of dispersion, I kept, even amidst the heavy rain, my standing-ground on the edge of the balcony. Ere long, with the suddenness of lightning, a rent was made in the curtain, an arm of the Tyri Fjord appeared, and then the whole groups of islands, with the remote mountains, and lovely cultivated intervening plains in picturesque confusion, the mist in some places holding on, in others rolling off, or up the ridge where I stood. It was hardly possible not to shout with delight, so enchanting was the effect, and so unlike anything I had ever seen before. The shimmering of the landscape through the mist was magical, and especially the effect upon water was astonishing. This was repeated, with an alternation of complete darkness and visibility, at least twice more, my anxiety being to watch where the light would unexpectedly appear, till at length, in one general retreat, the mist rolled back from the farthest mountains sixty or seventy miles off, only hanging upon the ridge on my right, at the upper end of the Steen Fjord, and leaving the whole hemisphere of distant mountain, plain, and lakes, with the village of Sundvolden and its fjord causeway far below— indeed, all that makes up the unrivalled Kongens Udsigt—revealed.'

A few miles further west, Drammen, a town most picturesquely situated on the Drammenselv, is reached. It is a busy, thriving place, of about 20,000 inhabitants, very largely occupied with the timber trade. The logs that are cut in the far-off Numedal, Hallingdal, Valders, and other wooded districts, float down the lakes, along the rivers, are tumbled unceremoniously over the falls, and, after reaching Drammen, are shipped to different parts of Europe and the United States. In this way timber to the amount of about £300,000 annually is exported.

Kongsberg, about sixty miles by rail from the capital, is noteworthy, not for any exceptional beauty of situation, but for its silver-mines, and as being the main approach to the Thelemarken district. It is the only region in Norway where as yet mining has proved really profitable. The conviction exists that other parts of the country would be found, on careful examination, rich in mineral wealth; but the absence of coal, and the almost insuperable obstacles to the carriage of heavy traffic, render Norway a most unpromising land for miners. But at Kongsberg for over 200 years the silver-mines have yielded a good return for the labour expended, and at the present time are worth about £22,000 a year.

There are two roads from Kongsberg to Tinoset. Travellers returning to Christiania usually go one way and return the other. Those who purpose crossing the Haukelid, or making their way to Skien or Christiansand, have to choose between the more beautiful scenery of the Bolkesjö route and the architectural attractions of Hitterdal. The landscape just before Bolkesjö Farm is reached is very celebrated. Du Chaillu says of it: 'I know of no farm in Norway so picturesquely situated, and none with such a peculiarly superb landscape. It is nestled among fir-clad hills, whose dark colour contrasts with the green meadows and fields which they surround. The place is partly hemmed in by barren mountains, on which are seen patches of snow. Everywhere little streams trickle down the hillside, filling the air with the sweet music of their waters.'

The other road passes along the north end of Hitterdals Vand and past Hitterdal Church, the only rival to the yet more noted Borgund Church. To the latter it is not considered equal as an architectural curiosity, but it is most probably of the same age, and certainly of the same style. The bell tower stands on the opposite side of the road. Bædaker satisfies the traveller's thirst for information about the building by the following compact statement: 'The style of architecture and general character of ornamentation of the singular Norwegian *stavekirker* relegate them to the twelfth century, the capitals of the pillars and the mouldings almost exactly corresponding, so far as the difference of materials allows, to the details of Anglo-Roman architecture at the same period. They are constructed, like block houses, of logs laid horizontally above each other, and kept in position by strong corner posts. The walls are surmounted by a lofty roof, the artistic construction of which was originally left open to view in the interior, though now, as in this case, often concealed by the interposition of a plain ceiling. The quadrangular nave is adjoined by a semicircular choir. Round the exterior of the building runs a low arcade, probably added as a protection against snow and cold; the lower part is closed, while the upper part is open and supported by small columns. Above the roof of this arcade appear the windows of the aisles, over which rises the nave, surmounted by a square tower with a slender spire. The windows of the aisle are an innovation, the original design having only small air-holes in their place. The capitals of the pillars, the doors and doorframes, and other suitable parts of the edifice, are embellished with elaborate and fantastic carvings, representing entwined dragons, intermixed with foliage and figures. The projections from the ridges of the roof and gables are also carved in grotesque forms.'

Hitterdal Church possesses among other curiosities a chair, wondrous in its carvings and of remarkable solidity. It stands by the altar, and is thought to date from about 900 A.D. If so, it is certainly one of the oldest chairs in existence.

Tinoset is a small village situated at the south end of the Tinsjö, a

HITTERDAL CHURCH.

lake about twenty-two miles long. A steamer runs to Strand, which is situated on the Maanelv, a little above the place where the river flows into the lake. About twelve miles from Strand the traveller reaches the approach to the great fall. A little way beyond the Krokan Inn, which is the property of the Norwegian Tourist Club, the first view of the cataract is obtained. It gets its name, which means the 'reeking' or 'smoking' fall,

THE RJUKANFOS.

from the fact that when a very large body of water is passing over the lower half is concealed by the dense clouds of mist and spray that rise up. The water falls over a height of 780 feet, that is, nearly twice as high as St. Paul's, and the appearance presented is all the more picturesque from the curious configuration of the chasm in which the fall occurs, and from the fact that it is impossible now to get very near. An old path, fit only for active and strong-nerved climbers, by which a closer view could be had, has been blocked up of late years as dangerous. The fall is well worth the time and trouble of the journey, though it is surpassed in the opinion of most by the stupendous falls of the Hardanger.

The old path that leads along the face of the precipice to a nearer view of the fall used to be called the Marie Stien, and a sad legend is connected with it. Many years ago, runs the story, the beautiful Marie of Westfjorddalen lived at her father's farm near the head of the fall. Her hand was sought by a wealthy lover, and her father favoured the suit, but her heart had long been won by the friend of her childhood, Ejstein Halfordsen. In those rude times deeds of violence were but too common, and the disappointed suitor formed a plot to waylay and murder his rival as he came one day to visit his betrothed. It came to the ears of Marie. How to warn Ejstein of his danger she knew not; but love is ingenious, and she boldly made the attempt to pass along the face of the cliff, the regular road being already occupied by the intending murderers. The effort succeeded. Marie warned her lover, and he fled the country. Years passed away; her father died, her enemy ceased to persecute, and, still constant, she lived in hope of the return of Ejstein. One day she thought she saw a figure approaching along the steep path which she had first discovered; it drew nearer; she recognised the features. It was Ejstein Halfordsen; he was returning, rich and honoured, to claim his bride. She ran to meet him. When he saw her he waved his arms and uttered her name with a glad cry of welcome. As he did so his foot slipped, he lost his balance, and fell headlong into the abyss below. Marie's intellect failed, and as she gradually faded away she would constantly walk up and down the narrow fatal path, and in fancy heard the voice of Ejstein mingling with the roar of the mighty waters of the Rjukanfos.

Dominating the whole region, and in full view of the fall, is the Gausta Fjeld. This mountain is the highest in Southern Norway, reaching an altitude of 6180 feet. It is not difficult of ascent, and a magnificent view over the whole Thelemarken country is obtained from its summit. The engraving facing this chapter shows well its pointed ridge and steep sides.

From Tinoset a fine road now leads over the Haukelid Pass to Odde, on the Sör Fjord. It has been but recently completed for carrioles, all travellers having formerly either to ride or walk over the pass. By this route the heart of Thelemarken is explored, many of the *stabburs* seen at the various farms, and in and about the houses much of the famous carving for which the region is famed. The most impressive views on the eastern side of the pass are found in Flatdal, as those on the western are in the Roldal. In our engraving a fine specimen of a Thelemarken house is shown. Du Chaillu thus describes a similar building: 'On the left of the entrance was a room about twenty feet square, with the usual open fireplace in the

FLATDAL.

corner, furnished with a large table painted red, a wooden bench, and a few oddly-shaped chairs, each made of the trunk of a tree; the windows consisted of small panes of glass. In two of the corners of the room beds had been constructed which resembled the bunks on shipboard. These bunks were gaudily painted, and the frame made fast to the ceiling, which was not more than eight feet high. A bright-coloured sideboard, as tall as the room, and fastened to the wall, contained plates, glass, spoons, &c. Facing the dwelling-house was the stabbur, probably over five hundred years old. I ascended a steep ladder to the upper storey, to which entrance was gained by means of an enormous key; the door turned upon strange-looking hinges, and the only light came through the fanciful open wood-work of the piazza. There was an aspect of the Middle Ages in the room, for everything in it was old and odd; the principal objects were huge chests, upon which were written the names of the owners. Each of the three daughters of the owner of the place had her own chest marked with her name, whose contents would form an important part of her dowry, in the shape of wearing apparel and trinkets. Upon cross-poles hung fourteen sheepskins as white as snow; women's skirts and dresses embroidered in silver, several table-cloths, with fanciful crochet-work at each end; and blankets of various bright colours were disposed about the room. The room below contained on one side large grain-bins placed close together; also stores of mutton, salted bacon, bags of flour, and baskets containing wool, some of which had been carded.'

From the earliest times carving has flourished in Scandinavia. The old Runic inscriptions are carved in stone. In many of the Swedish churches carvings both in wood and stone have survived, sometimes of the most quaint and curious kind, that go back six, seven, or eight centuries. The great Museum of Northern Antiquities at Copenhagen has a superb collection, and at the museum in Stockholm there are many splendid examples taken from ancient Swedish churches. In Norway also it seems to have been the custom from a very remote time to devote much attention to wood-carving. The churches of Borgund and Hitterdal are covered with this work. In many parts carved lintels and porches are to be seen. Thelemarken is especially rich in these products of native skill. The stabburs or storehouses are covered with this work, often of most intricate pattern and of cunning workmanship. Doorways are embellished with dragons of hideous aspect, and serpents of more than usually tortuous proclivities. Wooden forks and spoons and salt-boxes are often most elaborately ornamented. But the objects which perhaps most easily catch the eye and attract careful attention among the Norwegian household gods are the huge wooden tankards. These are everywhere to be met with, and often bear close scrutiny as to the design and execution of their carvings. Years ago it used to be easy to pick up splendid specimens of these in silver for a moderate price, but this rarely happens now. Our engraving exhibits some characteristic specimens of how the Norwegians can work in wood.

CARVED LINTEL, STABBUR AND TANKARDS.

The port of South Norway is Christiansand, and here almost all the steamers plying between England and Norway call. The entrance to the harbour is through a series of narrow passages between bare low rocky islets that look as if they had been ground down by the storms of ages. The town itself is prettily situated. The houses follow the general plan in being built of wood and arranged in long rectangular streets. They are clean and neat in appearance, and the windows filled with plants and flowers. The architectural feature of the place is the Cathedral, Christiansand, giving its name to a diocese. This building is now (1885) being rebuilt, the engraving depicting the tower as it used to be. In the harbour there are usually a number of steamers, and coasting and fishing vessels, but the

PART OF CHRISTIANSAND HARBOUR.

characteristic lack of bustle seems even more noticeable here than in the other considerable towns.

Christiansand is the easiest point of access for the Sætersdal, one of the most interesting and primitive regions of the country. In addition to the natural beauties, which are very considerable, this valley presents the most primitive buildings, while in habits and dress the inhabitants seem to have been wholly untouched by modern influences, and are now what their ancestors three or four centuries back were. The valley is not easy of access, and can only be seen by those prepared to take things as they are.

The food and sleeping accommodation are very plain, and sleep is sometimes a matter of difficulty to those who are disturbed by trifles.

The people are a powerful, well-made race, and their dress is to an English eye the most striking and unusual in the whole country. The women wear very short dresses, coming but a little below the knee; the skirts are of dark woollen material, ornamented with borders of gay colours. They also wear a profusion of the national silver ornaments, brooches, clasps, &c., and large copper belts of fine workmanship. The men array themselves in the high pantaloons reaching nearly up to the shoulder, and

VIEW NEAR STAVANGER.

correspondingly short waistcoats, upon which they display their silver ornaments. In Lower Thelemarken the costume is very similar, but the women wear longer skirts.

There is a good road from Christiansand to Ekersund, running through hilly and very pretty country. But as the journey takes about three days, while the steamboat does it in fourteen or fifteen hours, most travellers prefer to go by water. In South Norway the valleys branch out from the interior table-land to the coast on the east, south and west, and by reason of this peculiarity some who have explored this district, giving rein to their fancy, have compared the country to a pancake with split edges. Those who wish to see some of the loneliest regions of Norway, those most untouched by any foreign influence can gratify their curiosity to the full by making their way up these valleys. But those who go must be prepared and able to take care of themselves, as they will find but few of the accommodations to be met with along all the more frequented routes.

There is a considerable trade in fish between South Norway and England. Large quantities of mackerel are exported, packed in ice, and enormous numbers of lobsters. The Norwegians have vessels fitted up to carry the lobsters alive, resembling the plan adopted on the English cod-fishing boats for bringing in live cod. Large tanks are built in the ship's holds and into these the lobsters are placed while alive. And just as the North Sea trawlers like a fresh breeze and a little sea for their work, so these lobster boats prefer Neptune in a somewhat uneasy mood, for if it is too calm the lobsters all sink to the bottom of the tanks, and by crushing each other to death decrease greatly their market value.

Between Ekersund and Stavanger the steamers meet the full force of the North Sea, and by reason of the currents and the winds the passage is often a troubled one. These perils may be escaped by taking the train at Ekersund and travelling by rail to Stavanger, a distance of forty-eight miles. This is the only piece of railway in South-Western Norway.

The steamer on its way from Christiansand to Ekersund passes Cape Lindesnæs, or, as it is sometimes called, the Naze, the most southernly point of Norway. A lighthouse, 160 feet high, stands upon the Cape. Beyond Ekersund there is nothing striking along the coast until Stavanger Fjord is reached, where the unique West Coast scenery begins.

Stavanger, the other port of Southern Norway, is one of the oldest towns in the country, dating as far back as the eighth or ninth century. It is a place of considerable commercial importance, with a population of about 20,000. The steamers *en route* for Bergen call here, and the peculiar beauties of the west coast fjords are often first seen in the approach to Stavanger. The cathedral, second only to that of Trondhjem, dates from the eleventh century, was founded by an Englishman, Bishop Reinald, and is dedicated to the saint well known in London, and closely connected in popular report with the weather, St. Swithin, or, as he should be known, Suetonius, Bishop of Winchester, who departed this life A.D. 862. The building presents good specimens of the Norman and early Gothic architecture, and the choir is a fine example of the best thirteenth century building.

The environs of Stavanger are very beautiful, and a trip to the Lysefjord is well worth the time expended upon it. At Hafrsfjord, on the coast a few miles from the city, Harold Fairhair won the great victory in 872 over the combined forces of the Orkney and Norwegian earls that gave him the control and rule of the whole country.

Southern Norway has long been one of the most accessible districts of the country, but of late years the West Coast and the North Cape regions have proved more attractive to visitors. While none can deny the claims of these, it yet remains true that in Thelmarken, the Sætersdal, and the Stavanger Fjord, scenes of quiet beauty abound, and they possess distinctive features in the buildings, and in the dress and habits of the people, more strongly marked than in North Norway

A THELMARKEN STABBUR.

SOME HABITS AND CUSTOMS.

SUNDAY IN NORWAY.

GIRL SPINNING IN A SÆTER.

CHAPTER VII.

SOME HABITS AND CUSTOMS.

NORWEGIAN COURTESY—OWNERSHIP OF LAND—HOSPITABLE CHARACTER OF THE PEASANTRY—FARM-BUILDINGS—LIFE IN SÆTERS—MIDSUMMER EVE AND YULETIDE—PUBLIC WORSHIP—CONFIRMATION—WEDDING CUSTOMS—FUNERALS.

IN Norway, as in other European countries, the old habits and customs are fast disappearing, or altering under the influence of ideas spread abroad by education and contact with foreigners. In Christiania and Bergen, for example, the influence of London and Paris can be traced in the habits and dress of the people, and in the capital of Sweden is even more noticeable. And yet it is impossible to travel through any district of Norway or Sweden without observing many customs, habits and characteristics, never met with elsewhere. They are doomed, one feels, to serious modifications, but their banishment, and the substitution of other and more modern fashions would be, in almost every case, most unfortunate.

The Norwegians, as a people, are very courteous, kindly, and hospitable. They do all in their power to make visitors comfortable, and they do this, not in the hope of reaping a golden harvest, but because they consider it a duty to extend the courtesies of life towards the stranger and wayfarer.

It is greatly to be regretted that in some districts the constant stream of foreigners, who act towards the Norwegians upon ideas gained from travelling through Switzerland or Germany, is tending to modify the sturdy independence and entire absence of grasping desire hitherto maintained by the people. The only place where I saw begging children in Norway was along the magnificent Nærödal road, which is frequented by English and American tourists more lavish of their small coins than mindful of the best interests of Norwegian children.

Education and a direct interest in the soil are probably the most potent influences tending to produce and maintain the self-contained independence of the Norwegian peasant. The land is owned, not by a few wealthy proprietors, but by the bulk of the pepole. This, although it prevents the growth of a wealthy class, produces self-reliance and contentment. The peasants of Norway are better off, better educated, and, to all appearance, happier than the corresponding classes in any other European country.

On the death of a father all his property, real and personal, is divided equally among his children. Even if the owner of a farm sells it, by the law, as it stands, the next of kin has the right of buying it back, should he choose to do so within two years. Contrary to expectation, this custom has not led to such a subdivision of the land as to break it up into an enormous number of holdings, each too small to support the owner. The farms for the most part are of a fair size, and the people, on the whole, in comfortable circumstances. The number of paupers is very small, and the great extremes of wealth and poverty, such as obtain in England to-day, are almost unknown. The Norwegians are thoroughly democratic in their political views, the Storthing having as far back as 1821 abolished all titles, and the recent struggle between the Storthing and the ministry has ended in the victory of the popular views.

Having an interest in the soil, and being dependent entirely upon his own exertions, the ordinary Norwegian peasant is courteous to all men, and servile to none; he is willing to extend hospitality to all, and will rarely allow any return in the way of payment to be made; he is sufficiently interested in the outside world to display sometimes quite a naïve and embarrassing curiosity, and equally ready to satisfy to the extent of his power any desire for information possessed by his guest.

In both Norway and Sweden the writer was the recipient of kind acts of personal attention and hospitality to which his claims, judged from an English point of view, were very slight. The recollections of these are among the pleasantest memories connected with his Scandinavian experiences, since both Swedes and Norwegians have the knack of bestowing kind attentions upon a stranger in such a way as to lead him almost to feel that the debt is on their side, not his. The great bulk of the people belong to the bonder or peasant class. Speaking of these, and after considerable intercourse with them, Du Chaillu says: 'The Norwegian bonder is manly, self-possessed, and brave. Beneath his rough exterior he has a most kindly heart. He is truly and honestly pious, his religious feelings have been cultivated from his boyhood. In the character of both men and women is a vein of quietness and pensiveness, the result, no doubt, of the stern nature that surrounds them. The former are very clever at all kinds of handicraft. There is no country in Europe where the rites of hospitality are held more sacred. The traveller is surprised and delighted to see everywhere this beautiful trait in the character of the people.'

Norway is not a hopeful country for agricultural pursuits, and only about three per cent. of the land is under cultivation. Hay is the staple product. Barley, from which the ever-present *fladbröd* is made, and oats are the chief cereals. The abundant water is utilised for irrigation purposes by wooden troughs, and on nearly every farm a water-mill is found.

The farm buildings occupy three or four sides of a square. There is the house in which the family live, containing also the guest-chamber, another for the servants, a third for dairy and storehouse, and a fourth answering may be to an English barn. Around these, according to the size and work of the farm, sheds and out-buildings cluster. The roofs are often covered with earth, on which moss and flowers grow, and it is not at all uncommon to see a young fir plantation flourishing upon the roof of a farm building.

The interiors of the cottages, even of fairly well-to-do peasants, are to an English eye neither comfortable nor well furnished. There is but little furniture, the floor and walls, the chairs and tables, are generally plain wood. But they are often picturesque, and always full of interest to those entering them for the first time. The domestic utensils and appliances are generally rude in construction, but skilfully adapted for daily use. One feels that in these humble homes, the path of life is rough rather than smooth, and that if neither poverty nor riches there abide, the former is considerably the nearer, but that after all there is a healthy spirit of contentment and self-reliance not frequently met with elsewhere. A Norwegian cottage may not attract the visitor, but he cannot despise either the plain dwelling or the sturdy inmates.

A unique feature of Norwegian farm life is that part of it spent in the *sæters*. On the fjelds and lower slopes of the mountains during the summer months, there is pasturage for oxen, goats and sheep. One farm will sometimes own several hundred heads of cattle. The sæter is a rough wooden hut where those who look after the cattle sleep and have their meals. These are of course habitable only during the brief summer, and those upon whom this work falls usually go up to these mountain huts in the middle or end of June, and stay till the middle or end of September. Sæters are scattered about all over the country, often in very remote and out-of-the-way regions.

Life in a sæter is usually a very lonely existence. They are far from the farms, and for the most part difficult of access. The work is left mainly to the girls, two occupying each hut. During the day, whether it be wet or

INTERIOR OF A NORWEGIAN HOUSE.
(From a painting by Tidemand.)

fine, they tend the herds, milk the cows, and superintend the making of butter or cheese. The success or failure of their efforts frequently determine whether the ensuing winter will be one of comfort or of straitened means.

The most industrious occupy the rare leisure intervals by spinning wool, which is woven on the farms during the winter. Visits are few and far between. Provisions are brought up at stated intervals, and sometimes a friend or a lover will make a call, involving a toilsome journey of many miles. Many of the Norwegian girls pass the summer year after year in this lonesome, laborious life, and it is not wonderful that they seem to have less conversational tendencies than their sisters in other lands.

The Norwegians keep two main festivals, one at Midsummer Eve, the other at Yuletide or Christmas. The chief feature of the former is the lighting of bonfires. On my way to the North Cape I sailed up the west coast of Norway on that night a few miles south of Bodö. At intervals there would be two, three or four fires blazing on as many different hilltops in sight at one time, and we could see that each fire was surrounded by a crowd of gay merry-makers. In towns like Christiansund or Bergen, boats flit across the harbour, bonfires are lit on convenient islands and eminences, the people dress in holiday attire, bands of music abound, and the whole population seem to participate in a general rejoicing. In Sweden the day is observed in much the same way as the first of May used to be celebrated in the olden time in England.

The great festival of the year is the Yuletide. This, as we have noted in Chapter II., was one of the seasons observed in the old heathen days by sacrifices and revellings, and often by gross excesses and bloodshed. Christianity substituted a nobler subject of commemoration, and introduced more humane methods of observance. At the present day, making full allowance for the differences in the habits of the two nations, the Norwegian celebration of Christmas closely resembles the English. Falling in midwinter, when the work on the farms is light, and time can be spared, in many parts thirteen days are consumed in the round of gaieties. Parties are held, a general interchange of visits takes place, and many betrothals date from that happy period. Special attention is given to the brewing of the Yule ale, and all are expected to partake of it. Poor or rich, the household collects its best provisions in as bountiful a measure as possible, and great is the feasting. The cattle get double portions, and the birds are not forgotten, sheaves of oats, as shown in the engraving on p. 34, being fastened to the out-buildings. 'The day before Christmas,' writes Du Chaillu, 'in the afternoon, everything is ready; the house has been thoroughly cleaned, and leaves of juniper or fir are strewn on the floor. When the work is done the whole family generally go into the bakehouse, which has been made warm, and each member takes a thorough wash from head to foot, or a bath in a large tub—the only one many take during the year—then they put on clean linen, and are dressed. In the evening they gather round the table, the father reads from the Liturgy, and oftener a chapter of the Bible, and then a hearty meal is taken. In many of the valleys and mountain dales watch is kept during the whole of the night, and all are merry; candles are kept burning at the windows, and as in Dalecarlia, the people flock to church, each carrying a torch.'

There is much connected with the religious life of Norway that interests a stranger. In all parts of the country the ordinary wooden churches are found, and not unfrequently they are round structures, like those at Listad and Veblungsnaes. Owing to the mountainous character of the country, and the sparseness of the population, the churches are often far apart, and the worshippers have to come long distances. It is a pleasant sight either in the Hardanger, Valders, or Thelemarken districts, to see the peasants in

THE FINISHING TOUCH TO THE TOILET.

their picturesque costumes, all clean and fresh-looking, on their way to church. Those from a long distance come by stolkjaerre, or if dwelling on the shores of a fjord, by boat, the ride or the row extending sometimes over many miles. The women row quite as much as the men, and when the boat reaches the shore after a long pull, the finishing touch is given to the toilet, and each gives a friendly hand to the other.

The ordinary services are entirely free from anything approaching elaborate ritual. Liturgical forms are used, and in this respect the Lutheran Church is very conservative; but there is very little in Norwegian worship that in any way appeals to the sensuous side of human nature. In fact,

THE SCHOOLMASTER CATECHISING IN HITTERDAL CHURCH.
(From a Painting by Tidemand.)

there is much that conflicts with the English notion of what is appropriate for public worship. The buildings, even allowing for their quaint carvings and obvious antiquity, are as bald and unattractive as the oldest and plainest of meeting-houses. In many districts service is held only once in two or three Sundays. The result is, that the church is often crowded, and the ordinary service is followed by weddings, funerals, and baptisms. The priest is seen so seldom that he has long arrears to clear off when he does come.

The Norwegians, as a rule, are devout, simple-minded, and religious. They have a reverence for the printed page, and are fond of reading. Religious literature finds a ready and a wide circulation. The Bible is read at home, and many a Sunday hour is passed by the family in reading the Word of God. In Norway, the specially sacred part of Sunday seems to end early. This may be due in some measure to there being in most country districts only one service, and even where two are held evening services are rare. The custom has long obtained of devoting the closing hours of Sunday to dancing and to recreation. The writer, however, saw nothing in Norway corresponding to a Sunday in Germany or France.

Great stress is laid upon confirmation in the Norwegian Church. The clergy are not allowed to marry unconfirmed persons, and the rite is generally considered a necessary preliminary to securing a situation. The young people are trained carefully in Biblical history and in the Lutheran doctrine, and on the appointed day the priest lays his hands upon them. The examination, prior to the rite, usually takes place in the church, in the presence of the friends of the candidates. The schoolmaster sometimes undertakes this part of the work, and our engraving, from one of Tidemand's pictures, depicts a schoolmaster putting a class through the necessary examination in Hitterdal Church.

Human nature is much the same in Norway as in other parts of the world, and there, as elsewhere, love, courtship, marriage, and the habits and customs connected with them, play a very prominent part. Many of the popular tales bear upon this side of human life, some of them full of humour and sound common sense. One of the shortest and best we quote as it is given in Sir G. W. Dasent's *Popular Tales from the Norse*. It is called 'How One went out to Woo.'—'Once on a time there was a lad who went out to woo him a wife. Amongst other places, he came to a farmhouse, where the household were little better than beggars; but when the wooer came in, they wanted to make out that they were well to do, as you may guess. Now the husband had got a new arm to his coat.

'"Pray, take a seat," he said to the wooer; "but there's a shocking dust in the house."

'So he went about rubbing and wiping all the benches and tables with his new arm, but he kept the other all the while behind his back.

'The wife she had got one new shoe, and she went stamping and sliding with it up against the stools and chairs, saying, "How untidy it is here! Everything is out of its place!"

'Then they called out to their daughter to come and put things to rights; but the daughter she had got a new cap; so she put her head in at the door, and kept nodding and nodding, first to this side, and then to that.

'"Well! for my part," she said, "I can't be everywhere at once."

'Ay, ay! that was a well-to-do household the wooer had come to.'

Weddings in Norway, as elsewhere, attract a large share of attention, and present many novel and curious phenomena. The old customs obtain in full force only in the country districts, and even there are beginning to pass away. The betrothal, which takes place months or even years before the marriage, is a somewhat formal ceremony; it generally takes place on a Church festival, when the couple go before the clergyman, who asks them whether, in the presence of God and the witnesses standing by, they desire to be betrothed to each other. The affirmative answer being given, the couple exchange rings of plain gold, which are worn upon the ring-finger of the left hand. This is followed by the giving and receiving of presents. The man gives his psalm-book or jewellery and clothes, the women articles of wearing apparel that the betrothed must wear on the wedding day.

A NORWEGIAN BRIDE WEARING HER CROWN.

The wedding naturally is an event of the greatest importance, although some of the ancient festivities are nowadays being more honoured in the breach than in the observance. It frequently falls on a Sunday. The dressing of the bride, as in England, is one of the chief parts of the ceremonial. On the eventful morning she is escorted in procession by the bridegroom and his friends to the church, sometimes on foot and sometimes on horseback. On the return to the house of the bride's father, there is a great feast.

The great feature in the dress of the bride is the crown. This is usually made of silver, but is gilded, and hence has rather a fanciful appearance. These crowns are kept in certain districts, and lent to one and another as required. Mrs. Stone in *Through Norway in June* has described

N

A NORWEGIAN WEDDING.

two or three weddings which she witnessed with all a lady's quickness and completeness of observation.

'While standing among the guests,' she says, 'we heard the sound of music, and distinguished violins and a fife. Advancing towards us were three men, playing a slow and rather doleful tune, and behind them, walking with deliberate and measured steps, came the bridegroom and bride. The bride was decidedly plain. She wore a full skirt of black satin cloth, gathered all round the waist, and a bodice of the same material, the sleeves of a white bodice appearing from underneath the black. A black apron trimmed with fringe covered the front of the skirt. On her head was a wreath of artificial flowers of every colour under the sun, tied apparently by a couple of strings of coloured ribbon that fell down behind to her waist. Thick boots completed the costume. The crown, we learned, is being disregarded where the people consider themselves more fashionable. The groom was dressed in a blue cloth suit and a soft felt wide-awake hat, and reminded me of the skipper of a fishing-smack in his best shore-going toggery. The bridegroom wore a plain ring, as also the bride.'

The festivities usually last three days, spent for the most part in eating, drinking, and dancing. The bride generally keeps throughout the rejoicings to the dress in which the marriage takes place.

On another occasion Mrs. Stone saw four couples married at the same time. 'When all was ready the four bridegrooms came up to the chancel rails and stood around. The priest then addressed them collectively, and without a book; he next asked each a question, beginning with the men, to which an inaudible movement of the lips and a bow of the head was the answer given. The brides had rings on already before entering the church. After the questions asked and answered, each couple knelt with joined hands, and the priest announced in a form of words that they were married. The service was ended by all eight kneeling with bowed heads while the priest pronounced a benediction, accompanying it with the sign of the cross.

'The dress of the brides was most peculiar. Each wore a crown. These crowns are generally heirlooms, but if there be not one in the bride's family she procures one from a neighbour for the occasion. They are of beaten silver, but their appearance is entirely spoiled by being brassed over in parts in imitation of gold. This doubtless enhances their value to Norwegians, as silver is with them too plentiful to be held in much esteem. They were from four to eight inches high. One was entirely covered with brass; the other three looked older and showed in parts the silver. Two of them had silver pendants dangling about them, and three had either real or imitation stones inserted. The hair of each bride fell loosely down her back. Under the crowns and over the hair were pieces of ribbon about a yard long and a couple of inches wide. These spoiled the whole costume; they were of various colours, chiefly lilac and magenta. All the brides had bright scarlet skirts gathered fully round the waist. Over the skirts they wore embroidered white aprons. The bodices were short black jackets, covered in front with jewellery of all kinds, chiefly brooches of family silver, looking like breast-plates. White handkerchiefs finished the dressing at the neck. Each bride carried from three to five pocket-handkerchiefs in her hand.'

The happy human feelings so natural in connection with betrothal and marriage are manifest as strongly in Norway as in other parts of the world. Poetry, romance and folk-lore all cluster around this great turning-point in two lives. Dr. Jörgen Moë, afterwards Bishop of Christiansand, who assisted Asbjörnsen to make his famous collection of Norwegian Popular Tales, has thrown into graceful verse the tender side of the marriage relation in its beginnings. We quote the beautiful version given in Gosse's *Studies in Northern Literature*.

Now softly, lightly the evening dies,—
    Gold-red upon headland and waves without number,
And a soundless silence tenderly lies
And rocks all nature to dreamless slumber;
    Meadow and dingle
    Reflected, mingle
With waves that flash over sand and shingle
    In one dim light.

Ah! slim is the fisherman's boat, and yet
    High on the glittering wave it soars,
The fisherman bends to his laden net,
    While the girls are hushed at the silent oars.
    The soft emotion
    From vale and ocean
Has quenched the noise of the day's commotion,
    And bound it still.

And there stands one girl in a dream and sighs,
    While up to the clear warm sky she glances,
But full of longing her young thought flies
    To the Christmas games and the whirling dances;
    The deep red haze
    Of the evening blaze
Has thrown sparks farther than we can gaze—
    She sees afar!

Thou rich and rose-coloured summer night,
    Thou givest us more than the bright days bring;
O yield to beauty the best delight,—
    Let her dream come to her on gentle wing!
    While her boat caresses
    The low green nesses,
Lay the silver crown on her maiden tresses,
    As a happy bride!

GRANDMOTHER'S BRIDAL CROWN.
(From the picture by Tidemand in the Cartwright Gallery.)

The bridal party in many parts of Norway have to go and return to church by boat. When this is the case, the boats are gaily decorated, the fiddler takes his station on the prow of the first, and the rest follow in a procession. Sometimes the bride and her immediate attendants are rowed in a boat fitted up with something of the pomp and style of a state barge. At Christiansund on one occasion the author saw a small steamer sailing at full speed up and down the harbour, while those on board were firing off a small cannon at short intervals. This proved to be the rather noisy way chosen by a wedding party to celebrate that happy event. It did not strike one as the best way of commemorating a nuptial ceremony, but all on board the steamer seemed to be having what the Americans call 'a real good time.'

THE WEDDING PROCESSION.

The sorrows of humanity come as certainly and as surely to Norwegian hearts and homes as they do to other races in other lands. There are weddings, when all rejoice; there are funerals, when all weep. These also fall very frequently on the Sunday. To a large extent the pernicious notion that lavish expenditure is a fitting way of observing a funeral obtains in Norway. Relatives and friends come together. On the night before the funeral there is a feast of a solemn and decorous character. On the return from the churchyard, a grand feast begins which sometimes extends over three days.

The little that even a careful observer can see of the habits and customs of the people during a rapid journey through the country is enough to convince him that they are well worth careful study. The universal courtesy shown by taking off the hat alike to rich and poor, by the hand-shakings, and by the general demeanour, stands in pleasing contrast to much that is now common in England. There is little or none of the artificiality of modern life. As a people Norwegians are not given to extravagant displays of emotion, but they are fond of pleasure, and throw themselves very heartily into all customary ways of securing it. They welcome the coming guest, and they leave upon the mind of him who touches but the surface of their life the conviction that the better that life becomes known the more rich it will appear in qualities that call forth respect and admiration.

A GROUP OF DALECARLIANS.

FROM GOTHENBURG TO STOCKHOLM.

A VIEW IN SMAALAND.

GOTHENBURG.

CHAPTER VIII.

FROM GOTHENBURG TO STOCKHOLM.

GOTHENBURG—THE GOTHENBURG SYSTEM—SMÖRGÅS—ELSINORE—MALMÖ—SMAALAND—STOCKHOLM—UPSALA—LAKE MÄLAREN—THE GOTHA CANAL—MEM—BERG—MOTALA—WADSTENA—TROLLHÄTTA.

THE two chief towns in Sweden are the capital, Stockholm, and the port of Gothenburg. They have been brought into direct water communication by means of the Gotha Canal, which provides a waterway through the heart of the country, and removes the necessity for the longer sea-passage round the south of Sweden. The writer's first view of Sweden was gained from the deck of a Hull steamer as she was slowly passing up the Gotha River, the stream on which Gothenburg stands, at 5.30 on a June morning. The river winds along between rocky banks, and at every turn there are traces of the great timber trade of the country. The timber yards, the trim villas and neat cottages, the numerous craft, either moored or passing down the stream, the spires and buildings of the city as they gradually came into view, all helped to make a novel and pleasant picture.

On landing, the Dutch character of the town at once strikes the stranger. Wide canals run through the principal streets in the neighbourhood of the harbour, but the buildings resemble those of a French town. The town was founded by Gustavus Adolphus in 1619, and many Dutch settlers were among its first inhabitants. The great commercial prosperity of Gothenburg dates from the time of Napoleon I., when, owing to the Continental blockade, it became the chief port for the trade of England with North Europe. The Gotha Canal also, by bringing the town into easy communication with the interior of the country, has done much to make it prosperous.

Gothenburg possesses many fine streets and boulevards, and covers a large extent of ground. There are fine parks and public spaces, and the suburbs are occupied with large substantial-looking houses belonging to wealthy merchants. The people look bright and happy, and few towns give so favourable a first impression. The population numbers about 75,000.

Landing, as we did, on a holiday, a good opportunity was given us of studying the habits of the people, but the general closing of the shops and places of business did not allow us to see what the commercial activity of Gothenburg is like. We were most struck with the evident enjoyment taken by the people in simply walking and sitting about the beautiful Nya Allée, a fine walk with trees on either side, or along boulevards. In the afternoon the museum was opened free, and was visited by hundreds of men, women, and children. In the parks picnic parties were to be seen on all hands, and one could but feel that to all outward appearance this Swedish town compared very favourably in all respects with a large English town on a Bank Holiday.

The Gothenburg system of controlling the drink traffic, so called from the fact that it has been in force here for many years, seems to work very well. The municipal authorities license only a certain number of shops for the sale of pure and unadulterated spirits. These are in the hands of a company, who take five per cent. on their capital invested, and then hand over all the surplus profits to the town treasury, and they are used to lighten the rates. The managers of these shops have fixed salaries, and hence have no interest in urging their customers to drink. The system was extended to Stockholm in 1877. The system strikes the impartial observer as a sound one; it is also a fact that drunkenness has declined, and there are far fewer spirit 'bars' than there used to be. All the licensed shops close from 6 P.M. on Saturday to 8 A.M. on Monday.

At Gothenburg we first met the Swedish custom of *Smörgas* in all its native force. This is a dinner of relishes that immediately precedes the chief meal of the day. On a table in the dining-room are spread out a number of dishes containing bread, biscuits, butter, cheese, and such delicacies as raw salmon sliced, anchovies, raw salt herring, and various kinds of smoked meats. Decanters containing different kinds of strong spirit also adorn the board. The guests stand around the table; each spreads a piece of bread with butter and places upon it bits of the three, four, or five relishes he likes best, eats the compound, tosses off a small glass or two of the spirit, and is then ready for his dinner. The malicious say the whole process is an excuse for the glass of spirit. Those who never take spirits do not enjoy the custom, and on a first acquaintance the appearance and the odour of most of the dainties tend to take away rather than to stimulate the appetite.

There are several ways of reaching Stockholm from Gothenburg: by

ELSINORE.

rail, by canal, or by the circuitous route of steamboat to Copenhagen, and thence viâ Malmö to the capital. Choosing the latter route, we found the sail down the Sound exceedingly pleasant. We dropped down the river about 6 P.M., and all the evening we were sailing between the low rocky coast of Sweden and the low sandy shore of Denmark. Early the next morning we passed close by Elsinore, its ancient castle, on whose battlements Shakespeare made the ghost of Hamlet's father walk, standing out boldly and picturesquely in the morning sun.

Malmö is a busy little port, deriving its importance mainly from the fact that it is on the mail route between the chief cities of Denmark and Sweden. The railway journey to Stockholm is long and tedious, and is usually taken by night. In the summer months there is very little darkness, and the traveller unable to sleep will find it light enough to survey the chief points in the landscape. The first half of the route passes through the district called Smaaland, so named from the fact that it consists largely of small patches of arable land scattered over a wild, rocky and barren region. Mile after mile the train passes by lakes, forests, masses of rock, swamps and moors, fields of any size suited either for pasturage or tillage being very few and very far between.

Long ages ago the whole of Scandinavia was covered with ice and snow, and this region seems to have retained more numerous and clearer indications of ice action than many others. The rocks and boulders have been rounded and ground down by the tremendous friction of great glaciers in the remote past; great heaps of *débris* have been left here and there over the face of the country; bare rocks, wide stretches of land too thinly clad for cultivation, all testify to the former continuance of snow and ice. The landscape is monotonous and dreary as the train passes on hour after hour, but the traveller gets interested in watching the dark clumps of pine-forests, the stern and forbidding lakes, and the small cottages painted red, almost the only signs of human habitation.

The railway must have been an expensive construction, and needed skilful engineering. The difficulties of the country are very considerable, and the number of bridges, cuttings, and embankments are very great. Many travellers make their first railway journey in Scandinavia on this line. The carriages are comfortable, but the rate of travelling is very slow. It takes about fifteen hours to go from Malmö to Stockholm, a journey of 383 miles. Both in Norway and Sweden railway travelling is a very leisurely performance. No one seems in a hurry, and the stranger has ample time to study each station stopped at. In one respect the Swedish railways are far ahead of the English. The day trains stop for dinner, the night trains for supper at certain selected stations. On alighting, the traveller finds a good substantial meal of several well-cooked and smoking hot courses spread out in the dining room. He helps himself to all that he requires, finds tea and coffee ready on a side-table, has ample time to fully satisfy his hunger in perfect comfort, and the charge for the whole amounts to about two shillings.

After passing through the drear Smaaland district, the beauty of the country around Stockholm appears all the more striking. One who has fallen asleep after looking upon such scenes as those referred to above, and then wakes up near Stockholm, might be pardoned for thinking he had exchanged the wilderness for fairy-land. No city in North Europe rivals Stockholm for beauty of situation. This is due largely to the fact that it is built upon a collection of islands separated from each other by narrow and broad straits, most of the islands being rocky, well-wooded, and adorned either with public or mercantile buildings, or masses of beautiful trees.

Stockholm contains about 175,000 inhabitants, and while in some respects it justifies its claim to the title of the 'Venice of the North,' it is a cleaner and, in natural beauties, a more striking and picturesque city than its

RIDDARHOLM CHURCH.

namesake. The oldest part of the city is a group of three islands called Staden, Riddarholmen, and Helgeandsholmen, connected with each other and with the other islands on which the city is built by bridges. The bridge called the Norrbro, which leads to the island of Staden, forms one of the finest streets in the city, having the Hotel Rydberg at one end, and the huge square pile of the Palace at the other. One side is occupied by a row of good shops, and below the other is the Strömparterre, the most popular café. The Palace, built on an eminence, was begun in 1697, and finished in 1753. From the massive character of the architecture, and the height on which it stands, the building forms one of the most imposing objects in the capital. It also contains many splendid apartments, the chief being the great banqueting hall, known as 'the White Sea,' one hundred and thirty-five feet long, and one hundred and fourteen feet wide. The king's apartments and the queen's apartments are richly furnished, and filled with many interesting paintings, pieces of china, articles of *vertu*, and gifts from the various sovereigns of Europe.

Connected with Staden by a bridge is the Riddarholm, and from the centre of this rises an iron perforated spire, two hundred and ninety feet high, belonging to the Riddarholm Church,—the Stockholm Westminster Abbey. The building was originally possessed by the Franciscans, and was founded in the thirteenth century; but fires and restorations have very greatly altered it, and the spire is quite a recent erection. The church has long ceased to be used for any other purpose than as the royal mausoleum. On the walls are monuments to some of the early kings. The floor is paved with tombstones, and many celebrated men are buried beneath them. The most famous part is the Gustavus Adolphus Burial Chapel, built in 1633 in conformity with the plan drawn up by that monarch in 1629. The body of the great king was buried here after being brought by his soldiers from the fatal field of Lutzen, and now rests in the green marble sarcophagus standing on the south side of the altar, which has held it only since 1832. The sarcophagus was made in Italy by order of Gustavus III. for his father, but it reached Sweden only about 1830. Charles XIV. paid for it, and applied it to its present use. In the choir is a marble slab bearing the following inscription commemorative of the great Gustavus:

> In angustiis intravit,
> Pietatem amavit,
> Hostes prostravit,
> Regnum dilatavit,
> Suecos exaltavit,
> Oppressos liberavit,
> Moriens triumphavit.

This may be roughly translated, 'He braved dangers, loved piety, conquered his enemies, extended his kingdom, exalted his nation, set free the oppressed, and triumphed in his death.'

Many members of the present royal house are buried in this church.

A favourite point of view for overlooking Stockholm is a hill called Mosebacke, situated on the island of Södermalm, the southern quarter of the city. It is not very high, but the fatigue of reaching the summit has been minimised by the erection of a lift. A small payment gives the right of being taken up and brought down again. The hill is situated in the grounds o

STOCKHOLM.

of a café, but a small payment admits to a point of vantage from which a view unrivalled by any other capital in Europe is obtained. Spread out before the eye is the great metropolis, and a large area of the surrounding country. In the immediate foreground is the island of Staden, with the Palace and Riddarholm Church towering upon it; beyond these the Grand Hotel and the National Museum, and stretching away in all directions are the waterways, crowded with all kinds of craft, and wherever the eye turns a beautiful landscape of island, rock, water and foliage, bright and beautiful in the clear summer air under the bright summer sun.

The hotels of Stockholm are very fine, the chief being the Grand Hotel, which looks out across the harbour to the Palace. The view from one of the front windows on a light summer evening or on a moonlight night, when steamers are flitting to and fro across the water, when the lamps are alight in all parts of the great city and reflected in all directions by the ever-present waters, and with the enormous square palace dimly outlined opposite, is unique. Fine open spaces and cafés everywhere abound. The people strike the stranger as intelligent, easy-going, polite and fond of amusement. The gardens are thronged at all hours of the afternoon and evening, and vast numbers of the inhabitants seem to have nothing else to do than to sit listening to the music and sipping coffee or wine. The chief place of resort is Hasselbacken, on the island called Djurgarden or the Deerpark. The grounds are very pretty, they are thronged every evening with people, and refreshments can be had from a cup of coffee to a well-selected and beautifully-served dinner. Beyond the grounds of the café a winding road leads up through pine woods to a tower 110 feet high, called the Belvedere. From this point on a bright day a wide prospect of Stockholm and its environs is obtained.

Like other great European capitals, Stockholm offers much to interest various classes of observers. It has magnificent buildings like the National Museum, stored with antiquities from the Stone and Bronze Ages, and fine collections of ancient church carvings, and other objects well calculated to arouse the interest of the antiquarian; the lover of literature and the student of religious and philosophic thought can make a pilgrimage if so disposed to the house and study of Emanuel Swedenborg; the lover of the picturesque can see many a gay quaint costume worn by the peasants from different country districts; and to those who visit foreign climes for rest of body or brain, few cities present scenes and people more novel and more likely to catch the attention and arouse the interest than the Queen of the Baltic.

The environs of Stockholm afford a great variety of excursions either to scenes of great natural beauty or to buildings and places of historic interest. There are short trips to palaces like Drottningholm or Ulrichsdal, or longer ones up Lake Mälaren, or to the island of Gotland. The one possessing the most general interest is a visit to Upsala, the ancient capital of the country. It is situated on the river Fyrisa, and in remote times was the harbour and business centre of the royal town of Gamla Upsala, two miles distant. Upsala contains about 16,000 inhabitants, is the most famous University town in Sweden, possesses its most ancient cathedral, and is the centre of an archbishopric. It was a stronghold of paganism, and many heathen mounds and tombs yet remain in the neighbourhood. The strongest opposition to Christianity was exhibited and nourished here.

UPSALA CATHEDRAL.

Most visitors wend their way first to the cathedral, which, with its unlovely towers, forms the most prominent object in the town. It is a Gothic building, and, begun in 1289, was finished in 1435. Like most Scandinavian buildings, it has suffered much from fire, and in 1702 was very seriously damaged. The lightning struck and destroyed the three ancient towers four hundred feet high. The structure is very fine architecturally, consisting of a nave with aisles, a transept, and a choir. The chief interest centres in its monuments. On the north side of the altar is a sarcophagus said to contain the bones of Eric IX., the patron saint of Sweden, who died in 1160. Behind the choir is the fine Burial Chapel of

Gustavus Vasa, adorned with frescoes illustrative of scenes in the great king's life. He and his three wives are buried in it. In one of the chapels of the north aisle is the plain porphyry monument to Linnæus, whose remains are buried in another part of the church. The pulpit, which stands in the nave, is a wonderful erection, after a design by Tessin, and the sacristy contains a rich collection of relics, ecclesiastical jewels and ornaments, crowns, sceptres, and vestments.

The University was founded 1477, and endowed by Gustavus Adolphus. There are now fifty professors, and the students annually number about 1500. The library is large, containing 200,000 volumes and 7000 MSS. Among these the most interesting is the Codex Argenteus, that is, the translation by Bishop Ulphilas of the four Gospels into Meso-Gothic, dating from about 450 A.D. It contains 188 folios of parchment, and the letters are written in gold and silver. The MS. was captured in the Thirty Years' War, and was given by Christina, daughter of Gustavus Adolphus, to her librarian, who sold it to one of the Chancellors of the University for 400 crowns. Apart from its value as one of the minor evidences of the early text of the Gospels, it gives us almost all that is known about the early Gothic tongue.

LINNÆUS.
(From the Wedgwood Medallion by Flaxman.)

On a hill overlooking the town stands the castle, a plain, unattractive pile of building, begun in 1548 by Gustavus Vasa, but never finished on the original plan. Many incidents of interest and importance in the history of Sweden have happened here, notably the murder of Nils Sture, by order of Eric XIV., and the abdication of the eccentric Queen Christina, daughter of the great Gustavus, in 1654.

Gamla Upsala, about three miles distant, is famous for its *tumuli*, or ancient mounds. Three, known as the Tumuli of the Kings, each fifty-eight feet high, and two hundred and twenty-five feet in diameter, are called Thor, Odin, and Freyr, respectively. Near them is another, thirty-nine feet in height, called the Tinshög, or Assize Hill. From this hill the kings of

Sweden from very early times down to the age of Gustavus Vasa were in the habit of addressing their subjects.

All who wish for a pleasant excursion by water, and to combine with this some of the best and prettiest scenery in Sweden, should traverse the Gotha Canal in one of the canal steamboats. It is sometimes said that the scenery does not repay the two days and a half occupied by the trip. This was not our experience. The boats, it is true, are not very large, being limited to a length of 106 feet, the locks through which they have to pass not admitting larger vessels. The berths also give no more space than is absolutely necessary. Yet we found them very tolerable; the table is well

THE CASTLE AT UPSALA.

supplied, and the passengers are usually very pleasant. Swedes are very good linguists, and are very polite and willing to make themselves agreeable to strangers, so that an Englishman is almost always certain to find those on board with whom he can converse, even if he does not know a word of Swedish. The captains invariably speak English. In addition to this, the trip enables the traveller to see one of the greatest and most useful engineering achievements in Europe, and carries him from the Sound to the Baltic, brings him either from or to Gothenburg or Stockholm, and allows him to sail across Lakes Vener and Vetter, and presents many bright and beautiful scenes to his admiring gaze.

We left Stockholm about noon on a bright sunshiny June day in the steamer Balthasar von Platen, from the Riddarholm pier. The spire of the great church, the towers and domes and buildings of the capital, soon began to fade away into the distance, and were gradually shut out by the islands of Lake Mälaren. This lake is about seventy-five miles long, and is said to contain about 1400 islands. Sometimes they are large and well-wooded, with fine country houses and well-kept grounds; sometimes covered with pine-forest, the only sign of life being a labourer's cottage, or a little pier where timber is shipped; sometimes they are bare masses of rock. But under the bright sun, enlivened by passing steamers and boats, the lake is one of the most entrancing and delightful regions in Europe.

We carried about twenty cabin and fifty or sixty steerage or deck

ANCIENT MOUNDS AT GAMLA UPSALA.

passengers. Nearly all the latter were Finns on their way to the United States *viâ* Gothenburg, Hull and Liverpool. They are a much finer race physically than the Lapps, being taller, stronger, and better-looking, although there is little beauty among either the men or the women. Very large boots formed the most conspicuous part of the men's dress, and the women manage to have at least one red article of clothing. The fondness for this bright colour seemed universal. One of their number played what seemed to us very melancholy ditties on a kind of accordion, and we might have mistaken them for heartrending laments at leaving their native land, had not the general cheeriness and laughter rendered this idea incorrect.

After a couple of hours' sail along the lake the vessel turns southward, and by the Södertelge Canal passes out of Lake Mälaren into one of the almost countless arms of the Baltic Sea. This bay extends for fifteen or twenty miles, and presents scenery not unlike a series of Scotch lochs embosomed in a network of low hills instead of mountains. In all directions lanes of water open out, shut in sooner or later by rocky islets. Some of the islands were bare grim masses of stone, with only a few hardy trees growing in scattered clefts; others were completely covered with dense masses of trees, the foliage gleaming beautifully fresh and green in the afternoon sun. Towards the lower end of the bay the island Morkö is passed, on which, in a conspicuous situation, is the fine château of Horningsholm, built on the site of an ancient castle, which once belonged to

STEGEBORG CASTLE.

the great Sture family. The old castle was burnt down by the Russians in 1719.

After passing Morkö, for several hours the boat sails in a south-westerly direction, threading her way through the network of islands that here, as elsewhere in Scandinavia, fringe the coast. After passing Oxelösund, the Slatbakken, an arm of the Baltic running westward, is entered, and the scenery is very picturesque. We saw it under a fine sunset light, and the effect was most beautiful. We sailed slowly past the fine old ruined castle of Stegeborg, and on through a series of views of ever-varying beauty until we reached Mem, where we were confronted by the second of the seventy-five locks the steamer had to pass through before she can reach Gothenburg and the level of the Sound. These locks are well and solidly built, and occur at irregular intervals along the whole route of the canal. In all the steamer rises 308 feet above the level of the Baltic during her overland voyage.

A marble slab on the first lock at Mem bears the inscription, 'Except the Lord build the house they labour in vain that build it,' a not inappropriate motto for so great an undertaking as the Gotha Canal. Like other great projects, it was a hope and a scheme ages before it became an accomplished achievement. The fact of there being such large navigable lakes as Mälaren, Vener and Vetter led Bishop Brask of Linkoping (pronounced Linchipping, 'kop' in the Swedish having a sound something like the English word 'chip') to suggest the possibility of making a navigable route through the heart of the country. Gustavus Vasa and Charles IX. both looked favourably upon the scheme, but it was not until the eighteenth century that various attempts were made to construct the necessary works. Swedenborg and Polhem in 1716, and Viman in 1753 made strenuous efforts to overcome the difficulties at Trollhätta, but it was not until the year 1800 that what are now known as the 'old locks' at Akersvass were opened and the way made plain for vessels to pass from the Sound to Lake Vener.

The chief obstacle being successfully surmounted, the task of joining Lake Vener and the Baltic, for which surveys had already been made, was at once pushed forward. Baron Balthasar von Platen, aided by the English engineer Thomas Telford, settled in 1808 the final plans ; and the construction of the water-way, that can now be passed by the steamer in two days, occupied twenty-two years, from 1810 to 1832, and cost £280,000. Reckoning Polhem's efforts in 1716, the first really vigorous and promising effort to do the work, it occupied 116 years. But once done it was well done, and to the unscientific eye it seems as strong now as when first opened over fifty years since.

After passing three locks the steamer reaches Söderkoping, a town of 2000 inhabitants, and one that seems to have been of more importance in the fourteenth than in the nineteenth century. Between this place and Norsholm there are no less than eight locks. Fortunately we passed them at night, and as each lock occupies fifteen or twenty minutes, even if the steamer finds them empty and has not to wait for her turn, the passengers could sleep in comfort, knowing they were not missing the beauties of a great extent of country.

Norsholm is at the east end of Lake Roxen, which is about seventeen miles in length, and at the west end is the little hamlet of Berg. Here the locks form a gigantic staircase. There are no less than sixteen locks, by means of which the steamer is lifted up 120 feet. We reached Berg about 7.30 A.M., and as the breakfast bell did not ring until nine o'clock, and as it takes several hours for the steamer to climb the lock staircase, most of the passengers went for a morning stroll. One charm of this trip is that at places like Berg and Trollhätta the steamer can be left with safety, and one, two or three hour trips, as the case may be, made on land. We visited Wreta Church, which is situated in the midst of pretty rural country, and which contains some curious ancient monuments.

After rejoining the steamer, we traversed a part of the canal built somewhat above the level of the country, and enjoyed the novel experience of sailing along high above a wide and level expanse of pretty country. Lake Boren, nearly ten miles long, is next traversed, and forms one of the finest stages of the journey. At Borenshult there is a five-lock staircase, rising forty-nine feet, and giving those who desire a little exercise the opportunity of a walk to the next stopping-place, Motala. On the way a large iron-works situated on the bank of the canal is passed. Baron von Platen, after whom the steamer in which we journeyed was named, is buried here, at one of the most interesting parts of the great construction to which he gave many of the best years of his life.

Motala is a place of some importance, and is very prettily situated. It forms a kind of half-way house between Stockholm and Gothenburg, the total distance being 259 miles. Old women come on board with good specimens of Swedish lace, and the vendors of various kinds of merchandise try to push trade while the steamer tarries.

About an hour's journey from Motala, Vadstena, on Lake Vetter, is reached. Hard by the landing is the Vettersborg, a fine old castle dating from the sixteenth century. An engraving of it is given on page ix. A violent thunder-storm came on while we were here, and interfered considerably with our enjoyment of the scenery. It rained heavily for a large part of the time occupied in crossing Lake Vetter, the steamer sailing nearly due east, and thus crossing the shortest diameter of the lake. The canal is regained at Carlsberg, a fortress never completed, having been begun in 1820. The situation is very beautiful, and the contrast to the wide sheet of water just crossed was very interesting. The ascent of a solitary lock, the thirty-seventh since starting, admitted the steamer to the picturesque Lake Viken, the highest point of the route above the sea.

At the east end of Lake Viken the descent towards the Sound begins. Except for Trollhätta, the western half is much less interesting than the eastern. At Toreboda the railway line between Gothenburg and Stockholm is crossed, and a few miles farther the wide waters of the great inland sea known as Lake Vener are touched. On reaching the deck in the early morning, my first impression was that we were out at sea. On three sides of us no land at all was in sight, and away in the south-west, the direction of our course, it was only a faint blue outline in the far distance. The lake is 100 miles long, and at its widest part, viz. where the canal enters it, 50 miles across. It has an area of 2200 square miles, and stands 143 feet higher than the sea. The large rivers of the interior of Sweden drain into it, and the timber is floated down in great rafts to Venersberg, and thence by the Gotha River to the sea. It is a troubled sheet of water, as often in a stormy as in a peaceful mood, and if the traveller is to have 'a bad quarter of an hour,' he usually gets it here. Fortunately the breeze was blowing in the direction we were steaming, and we were able to make a good breakfast in peace and quietness.

At noon we reached Venersborg, a town of about 6000 inhabitants, situated at the southern end of the lake, where its waters pour forth and form the Gotha River. It is a great centre for the lake and canal steamboat traffic, and is a busy little place. A short sail down the river brought the Balthasar von Platen to Trollhätta, where, as I intended staying the night, I had to bid farewell to the courteous captain and the pleasant acquaintances formed during the two days' sail. My account for two days, the items entered by myself, after the Swedish fashion, in a book provided for the purpose, *including* fees, amounted to only sixteen shillings and fourpence. Considering that the fare was plentiful and good, this could not be considered very exorbitant.

I had heard so much of Trollhätta that I wished to give the place a leisurely inspection, and the more I saw of its wonders and beauties the more fascinating they appeared. The falls exhibit no scene comparable to the Skjæggedalsfos in volume, nor do they tumble from a height that is in itself impressive. They consist of a series of tremendous rapids spread over a distance of about two hundred yards. The great impression produced by them is one of terrific resistless force. As the wild waters rush by with tremendous uproar, one has the feeling that no power short of Omnipotence could stay them in their mad onward rush.

The first fall is only twenty-three feet high, but is certainly one of the most striking. Saw-mills and works whose machinery is driven by the water power line the east bank of the falls. From a platform attached to one of these you can reach a point only a few yards distant from the rushing water. Looking up the current, you see the Gotha River, which seems, to one who knows that away in the distance it is fed by the exhaustless waters of Lake Vener, a more imposing river than it really is. It is at this point a fine broad stream. The surface is smooth, the current is running with a terribly accelerating velocity, the colour is a bright clear green, and just where the platform is fixed the ridge of rock begins to slope. The mass of water, looking like glass suddenly endowed with flexibility, bends in a smooth unruffled sheet over the first four or five feet of the fall, and then breaks with a crashing roar into a wild sea of foam and spray and surging waves. Right in the middle of the fall is the island of Gullö, and the water dashes down upon this as if to sweep it away, and, failing in this, surges away on either side and goes thundering on to the next fall. I have never seen a more fascinating object than the swiftly moving, unbroken sheet of clear water bending over the brink of the fall.

Lower down, after passing through part of a saw-mill and paying a small fee, the visitor is allowed to cross a narrow bridge that spans the second cataract, and allows him to reach the little island of Toppö. It really needs a strong nerve to stand on the centre of the bridge and enjoy the wild scene. As shown in the engraving, the water rushes down with fearful velocity. Immediately beneath the bridge the water falls for a depth

TOPPÖ FALL, TROLLHÄTTA.

of forty-two feet. The noise is deafening, and the certainty of what would be the fate of any one who should fall from the bridge into the seething waters makes the observer uneasy lest the bridge, which looks none too strong, should give way while he is on it. The island of Gullö is shown in the background, and by the two distant bridges access is gained to the hill on the right bank, from which a very fine view of the whole range of the cataracts is obtained.

The water forms wild rushing cataracts on either side of the islands Gullö and Toppö, then rushes onward in a series of minor falls until the level of the river is reached. There is a very fine walk along the left bank of the stream, and it is hard to believe that the placid, easily flowing stream is formed of the water that has only just made the furious descent of the rapids. The path winds along through fir and pine trees, affording here and there picturesque views. Hard by the main falls the old half-completed locks, begun by Polhem a century and a half ago, are still to be seen. The water has long found its way into them, and the chief one, called Polhem's Sluss, might easily be mistaken for a natural fall.

THE NEW LOCKS AT AKERSVASS.

About two miles and a half below Trollhätta, the last series of locks on the canal are situated at a place called Akersvass. It is a beautiful spot, well wooded, having pretty cottages dotted about, and with the fine river ever flowing past towards the sea. Here the problem of constructing the canal was practically solved by the completion of the locks that enabled vessels to pass by the formidable Trollhätta Falls.

The first attempts were unsuccessfully made higher up the river, but in the year 1800 a series of eight locks were built, and they are still used, but are available only for small vessels. During the years 1836 to 1844, Ericson built a series of eleven large locks, which are now in daily use for the steamers and heavy shipping. The engraving shows the beginning of the ascent, where the level of the Gotha River is being left.

On a fine afternoon, like the day on which we saw it, few spots in Sweden are so pleasant for a ramble as this. The engineering work well repays careful scrutiny. It is interesting to watch the vessels ascending or descending. The walk along the bank up to the top of the ascent is very pretty. The view is very fine, and the walk back to Trollhätta by the banks of the canal very enjoyable.

Late on in the evening I wandered about the main falls, which presented very beautiful colour effects in the soft pinkish-golden light of the sunset. The roar of the water is ever audible, loud and even deafening as you stand near one of the main cataracts, and like the noise of the sea on a pebbly beach at a distance. Strolling about and walking along wherever gates and fences did not bar the way, I fell in with an amateur guide in the person of a young clerk engaged in a large iron-works that stands by the Gullö Fall. His English was not perfect, but he was glad of an opportunity to practise that speech with a native. With the ready Swedish courtesy, he did his best to point out to me the features of special interest met in our walk; and when he found I was really willing to give him what aid I could, he got me to pronounce a number of English words that he had found stumbling-blocks. He explained that, as there was so much trade between England and Sweden, it was essential that he should master that language if possible. He did not think it an easy task; but if he approaches all English travellers he meets with the polite persistence he manifested towards me, I feel certain that success will reward him at last. The incident interested me, because it exhibited at once the national politeness and also their intense desire to master the somewhat difficult English language.

My evening ramble ended where my afternoon one began—on the platform overlooking the top of the first or Gullö Fall. I seemed drawn by a strong fascination to that wide belt of water which looked like a sheet of green glass gliding by with immense velocity, and which seemed as if it must draw one into its fatal current. Seen in the quiet evening light under the influence of these sensations, one can readily understand how the Scandinavian mind has from time immemorial peopled the region with 'trolls,' those dull-witted curious creations of Norse fancy, mighty in strength, but inferior to man in mental subtlety and power. It will be long indeed before the impression of force made upon the mind by the mad swirl of the waters around the island Gullö will be weakened or effaced.

The next morning the train conveyed me to Christiania, a distance of one hundred and seventy-five miles. We travelled securely and had ample time to survey the country, but the rate of progress seemed very slow to one accustomed to English railways. It took twelve hours to reach the Norwegian capital. At one point very fine views of Lake Vener are obtained; at Sarpsborg the train passes almost immediately over the falls there formed by the Glommen; and on nearing Christiania a wide sweep of the surrounding country and of the great fjord is in full view from the carriage windows. On bidding farewell to Sweden, one cannot help feeling that, although for natural beauty it must yield the palm to Norway, it is yet well worth a visit, and that Stockholm, Trollhätta and Smaaland possess individualities sufficiently strong not only to delight and interest the traveller when he first sees them, but also to abide in the memory even after the sight of the midnight sun or the sombre heights of the Naerödal.

MOTALA.

A View in North Sweden.

INDEX.

AN attempt is made in the following Index to give roughly the pronunciation of those Norwegian names and words that are most likely to appear strange to an English eye. For any one not familiar with Norse, it is only possible to do this approximately. A few general rules may be stated here, and they will be found to cover almost all the cases that present any difficulty.

1. *J* is pronounced like the English *y*: e.g., 'Jondal' is pronounced 'Yondal.'
2. *K* before *e, i, j, y*, and *ö* is pronounced like the English *ch*: e.g., 'Kjelstadli' = 'Chelstadli,' 'Söderköping' = 'Söderchipping'; *sk* = *sh* before the same vowels: e.g., 'Skjæggestad' = 'Shěggěstad.'
3. *A, e*, and *i* have respectively the sounds of *a* in father, *e* in there, and *i* of *ee* in sheen. *Aa* has the sound of *oa* in Oak: e.g., 'Aak' = 'Oak,' 'Aalesund' = 'Oalesund.'
4. *Ö* has the sound of the German *ö*: e.g., 'Vöringfos' = 'Věringfos.'
5. *U* in proper names is generally long, and has the sound of *oo*: e.g., 'Aalesund' = 'soond.'
6. Many words commonly used as parts of names have distinct meanings: e.g., *dal* = valley; *elv*, river; *fjeld*, mountain; *fjord*, arm of the sea; *fos*, waterfall; *gaard* (*gōrd*), farm-house or yard; *klev*, cliff; *nut*, peak; *næs*, cape or promontory; *sund*, strait; *vand*, water or lake; and *ö*, island.

AALESUND (Olesound), trade of, 115
Aardal, 150
Aardals Fjord, the, 150
Aardalsvand, the, 150
Akers Church, 93; Hauge's grave in, 95
Akers-Elv, the, 88
Akers Hus, 95
Akersvass, locks at, 217
Athelstan and Harold, relations between, 31
Arctic Circle, the, farewell to, 84

BÆGNA river, the, 158
Bakke fall, the, 153
Balholmen, beauty of, 150
Bears, travellers' acquaintance with, 17
Bergen, arrival at, 124; description of, 126; trade of, 126; inhabitants of, 127; education at, 127; houses at, 128; museum at, 128; railway at, 131
Berg, lock-staircase at, 213
Bishops, appointment of, 18
Björne Fjord (Byěrně), the, 131
Blanflaten (Blöflåten), station at, 153
Bolkesjö (Bolchesyě) route, beauty of, 165
Bonfires on Midsummer Eve, 183
Boren, Lake, 214
Borenshult, 214
Borgund (Borgoond), Church of,153
Bredevangen, description of, 104; amount of hotel bill at, 104
Bredheims Vand, 121
Buarbræ glacier, the, 134

CARL JOHANS GADE, the, 88
Carlsberg, 214
Carriole, the, description of, 24, 101
Carving, Scandinavian, 171

Christiania Fjord, the scenery of, 163
Christiania, description of, 87; the Carl Johans Gade at, 88; palace at, 88; university of, 89; Viking's ship at, 89; Church of the Trinity at, 92; Akers Church at, 93; Town Hall of, 93; life of Hauge at, 93; Storthings Hus at, 95; Oscar's Hall, near, 96
Christiansand, situation of, 173; houses of, 173; cathedral at, 173
Christiansand Harbour, 172
Christiansund (Christiansoond), description of, 113
Christmas or Yuletide, ancient customs at, 33; modern customs at, 183
Cottage interiors, 181
Courtesy of Norwegians, 179
Cnut, career of, 40
Church Government, form of, 18
Churches, services in, 21; furniture of, 21
Clergy, appointment of, 18; dress of, 21
Cod fishery, the, extent of, 61
Colporteur among Lofoten fishermen, report of, 61
Confirmation, rite of, 187

DANCING at Odde, 141
Dinner at Skjæggestad (Shěggěstal), 102
Dombaas (Dombös), station of, 104
Dovrefjeld mountains, botanical treasures of, 104
Drammen, timber trade of, 164
Drottningholm, palace of, 207

EDUCATION in Norway, 23; at Bergen, 127
Egeberg (Egěbairg), the, 88
Eid Fjord, the, 143
Eide (Eidě), 133; beauty of, 145
Lidsvold, 97
Eidesnut (Eiděsnoot), the, 134
Einar, the archer, 37

P

Einsætfjeld (Einsaitfyeld), the, 140
Ekersund, 174
Eric Blood-Axe, career of, 32
Espelandsfos, the, 135
Ethelred, attack of, on London, 39

FAGERNÆS, station at, 157
Fairhair, Harold. *See* Harald Haarfagre.
Faleide (Faleidē), beauties of, 121
Farm buildings, 181
Farms on the cliffs, 121
Fille Fjeld (Fillē Fyeld), the road over, 153
Fin the archer, 37
Finmarken, 81
Finn emigrants, 211
Fjeld, etymology of, 16
Fjeldstue, a, 156
Fjärlands Fjord, the, 150
Fjord, etymology of, 16
Fladbröd (Flabbro), 181
Flatdal, views in, 168
Flowers, profusion of, at Trondhjem, 48; at Molde, 114
Fog, stopped by the, 56; hindered by, 144
Folgefond, the, 16
Folgefond glacier, the, 131; fine view of, 139
Franchise, the, description of, 23
Free Churches, description of, 21
Frithiof, the inheritance of, 150
Frognersæter, 96
Funerals, 195
Frydenlund, 158

GALDHÖPPIGGEN, the, height of, 16
Gamla Upsala, mounds at, 209
Gausta Fjeld (Gösta fyeld), the, height of, 168
Geiranger Fjord, beauty of, 118
Gimsö Strom, description of, 63
Gjövik (Gyervik, *gy* being sounded almost like the French *ch* in *chère*), scenery of, 98
Glacial action, signs of, in Sweden, 202
Glaciers of Norway, 16
Glommen, the course of, 16
Gokstad, discovery of Viking's ship at, 90
Gotha (Göta) Canal, the, 199, 210
Gothenburg (Gottenberg), history of, 199; streets of, 200; people of, 200; licensing system at, 200; custom of *Smörgas* at, 200
Gotland, island of, 207
Government in Norway, form of, 22
Gravens Kirke, descent to, 145
Gravens Vand, 145
Griffenfeld, Peter, prison of, 53
Grindaheim, 157
Gudbrand, conversion of, 41
Gudbrandsdal (Goodbrandsdal), the, description of, 101
Gudvangen (Goodvangen), situation of, 148
'Guest's Wisdom, The,' quotations from, 30
Gullö, Fall at, 216
Gustavus Adolphus Burial Chapel, Stockholm, 204

HÆG, the, road at, 155
Hafrs Fjord, battle at, 31
Hakon, son of Sigurd, rule of, 34
Hakon before Athelstan, 32; baptism of, 32; rule of, 32
Halfdan the Black, rule of, 30
Halgö, island of, 98
Hamar, description of, 98
Hammerfest, description of, 76
Harald Haarfagre (Harald Hörfägre), or Harold Fair-hair, story of, 30
Hardanger Fjord, the, area of, 17; the scenery in, 131, 132
Hardanger peasantry, the, 132
Harstadhavn, description of, 64

Hauge (Howge), Hans Niel, sketch of, 93
Hauk Hanbrok before Athelstan, 32
Haukelid Pass, the, 133
Helgeandsholmen, 203
Hellesylt (Helleseult), 121
Henningsvær, description of, 58
Hindö, island of, 63
Hitterdal Church, description of, 165
Hjelder (Hyelder), places for drying fish, 81
Hornelen, the cliff, 116
Hönefos (Hēnefos), situation of, 159; sawmills at, 160
Honingsholm, Château of, 212
Horgheim, mountains near, 109
Horningdalsrokken, height of, 121
Hospitality of Norwegians, 180
Hovestnen, or Hove Cottage, 96
'How one went out to woo,' 187
Husum (Hoosum), 153

INVIK FJORD, view over, 122

Jägts (Yats), 113
Jarls or earls (yarls), lordship of, 30
Jolstervand (Yolstervänd), 122
Jondal (Yondal), situation of, 132
Jordalsnut (Yordälsnoot), the, height of, 146
Jostedal Fond, the, 16
Jostedals glacier, 149
Jostedalsbræ, 122, 150

KALDAFJELD (Käldafyeld), the, height of, 146
Kilfos (Keelfos), the, 146
King of Norway, the, powers of, 22
King's View, or *Kongens Udsigt* (Konyens Oodseet), 164
Kjelstadli (Chelstadlee), station at, 121
Klipfisk, or dried cod-fish, 114
Kolbein Sterki and the idols, 41
Kongsberg, mines at, 165
Krokan Inn, the, 167
Krokleven, view from, 164
Kvindherreds Fjord, the, 131

LADE, village of, 54
Lærdalsören, 150, 153
Læra, the, course of, 153
Land, ownership of, 180
Lapps, encampment of, 65; description of, 65; treatment of babies at, 66; reindeer at, 66; etymology of name, 70; races of, 71; travelling of, 71; character of, 72; church services of, 75
Laghing, the, description of, 23
Lendogarde, island of, 57
Lerfos, Greater and Lesser, the, 54
Lesjeskogen (Lesyeskögēn), Vand, the, 104
Licensing system of Gothenburg, 201
Lillehammer, description of, 98
Lindesnæs, Cape, 175
Listad, post station at, 102
Lobsters, abundance of, 17; trade in live, 175
Lödingen, hamlet of, telegram at, 63
Lofoten (Lofōten) Islands, the, description of, 58; fisheries in, 58, 59
Loksund, beauty of, 131
London, attack on, by Olaf, 39
Long Serpent, the, 36
Lotefos (Lotēfos), the, 135
Lougen, the river, 102
Lyngenfjord, the, description of, 82
Lyseford, the, 175
Lyster Fjord, the scenery of, 150

MAABODAL (Mobödäl), the, 143
Maanelv (Mönelv), the, 167
Magerö Sund, the, 77

Magpie, the, 17
Mälaren, Lake, 211
Malmö, 202
Marie Stien, the legend of, 168
Maristuen, 155
Mel Fjord, the, 83
Melderskin (Meklersheen), the, 132
Mem, locks at, 213
Merauk (Merök), 118
Meridianstötte, the, at Hammerfest, 77
Mesna, the, falls on, 98
Midnight sun, the, duration of, 15; beautiful sight of, at Vaags Fjord, 63
Mjösen (Myösen) Lake, area of, 16; description of, 97
Moen, 150
Mogelifos, the, 139
Molde, beauty of, 114; flowers at, 114
Molden, harbour of, 115
Mölmen, 107
Mongefos, the, 108
Morkö, island, 212
Mosebacke, view of Stockholm from, 204
Motala, situation of, 214
Mountain Lapps, description of, 71
Multeberry, the, 102
Munkholmen, island of, at Trondhjem, 52

NÆRÖ FJORD, the, scenery of, 150
Nærödal, the, 146
Nedre Vasenden, farm at, 122
Nidaros, or Trondhjem (Tronyem), foundation of, 36
Nid Elv, the, 55
Nord Fjord, the, scenery of, 116
Nordkyn, description of, 80
Norheims Fjord, the, 133
Norrbro bridge, Stockholm, 203
Norse influence on England, 29; literature, 29
Norse tale, 187
Norsholm, 213
North Cape, the, description of midnight at, 79
Norway, area and population of, 15; geology of, 16; fjords of, 16; mountains of, 16; rivers of, 16; lakes of, 16; waterfalls of, 17; fauna of, 17; flora of, 18; climate of, 18; religion of, 18; Free Churches of, 21; constitution of, 22; legislature of, 23; education in, 23; railways of, 24; carriages of, 24; impressions of, 24
Nystuen (Neestuen), description of, 156

ODDE (Oddë), situation of, 133; peasant dancing at, 141
Odelsthing, the, description of, 23
Odnæs, hotel at, 158
Oifjords (Oifyords) Vand, the, 143
Olaf the Saint, story of, 39
Olaf Tryggveson (Oläf Treugveyson), story of, 33
Opheims Vand, the, 146
Ormeim, 108
Oscar's Hall, description of, 96
Oscar II., character of, 23
Ovre Seim, station at, 145

PINE FORESTS, 18, 146, 158
Porsanger Fjord, the, area of, 17
Ptarmigan, plentifulness of, 17

RAFT SUND (Raft Soond), the, description of, 63
Railway journey from Malmö to Stockholm, 202
Railways in Norway, 24
Rainfall of Norway, the, 18
Randsfjord, the, area of, 16; description of, 158
Rauma, valley of the, description of, 107
Red, view at, 122
Reindeer, uses of, 66; travelling with, 71
Riddarholm Church, description of, 204

Riddarholmen, 203
Ringedals Vand, 121; description of, 139
Rjukanfos, (Ryukanfos) the, 163; description of, 167
Rippa or *rype* (reupë), the, 17
River Laps, description of, 71
Roads of Norway, the, 24
Roldal, views in, 168
Rolf the Ganger, story of, 31
Romsdal Horn, the, approach to, 109
Rosendal, 132
Row-boat, travelling by, 121
Roxen, Lake, 213
Rusten, Pass of, description of, 104

SÆTERS (Sayters), description of, 181
Sætersdal (Saytersdal), the, description of, 173; people of, 174
Sagas (Sägas), the, quotations from, 29
Salmon, abundance of, 17
Sand Vand, the, 133
Sarpsborg, 219
Sea Lapps, the, description of, 71
Seven Sisters, the, 57, 83
Seven Sisters Fall, the, 118
Sevlefos, the, 148
Sigrid the Haughty, story of, 36
Skjæggedalsfos (Shëggëdalsfos), the, visit to, 135
Skjæggestad (Shëggëstat), dinner at, 102
Skate Sund, the, 116
Skjervefos (Shervëfos) the, 145
Skjervet (Shervet), valley of, road in, 145
Skogstad, the, 157
Skydsgut (Shisgoot), the, 102
Slatbakken, the, scenery, of, 212
Slettafos, the, 108
Smaaland (Smöland), description of, 202
Smörgas (Smergäs) custom of, at Gothenburg, 200
Snehätten, the, height of, 16
Söderköping (Söderchipping), population of, 213
Sogne Fjord (Sonë), the, area of, 17; scenery of, 148
Sognefest, the, 149
Sör Fjord, extent of, 131
Stabburs, 168
Staden, island of, 203
Stadt headland, the, 124
Stalheim, 148
Stalheimsfos, the, 148
Stalheimsklev, road at, 147
Stang, Frederick, funeral of, 92
Stavanger, description of, 175
Steamers, description of, 54
Stiklestad, battle of, 43
Stockholm, beauty of situation, 202; population of, 203; streets of, 203; palace at, 204; Riddarholm Church at, 294; hotels of, 207; attractions of, 207; environs of, 207
Stolkjærre (Stolkyerrë) the, description of 24, 101
Storthing (Storting) the, description of, 23
Strand, steamer to, 167
Strandefjord, the, 158
Stueflaaten (Stuefloten), scenery at, 108
Sunday observance, 187
Sunday service in Lapland, a, 75
Sunelvfjord, the, 121
Sværholtklubben (Svairholtkloobben), the, description of, 78
Svartisen (Svartcesen), the, 16, 83
Sweyn Forked-Beard, career of, 36

TEMPERATURE of Norway, the, 18
Terö, island of, 131
Thelemarken (Telemarken), description of, 168
Thorwaldsen's (Torvaldsen) statue of the Saviour, 51
Throndenæs (Trondenæs) Church, 64

INDEX.

Tklemand, description of paintings by, 96
Tides, height of, 18
Timber trade at Hönefos, 160; at Drammen, 164
Tinoset, 166
Tinsjö (Tinsyo), the, 166
Tjall (Tynll) Sund, the, 63
Toppö, fall at, 216
Toreboda, 214
Torghätten, description of, 57
Torvet, or market-place at Bergen, 125
Trade with England, 175
Tract distribution in Norway, extent of, 21
Trefoldigheds Church, description of, 92
Trollhätta, description of, 25
Trolltinderne (Tröltindërnë), or the Witch-Pinnacles, 109; legend of, 109
Tromsö, description of, 64; Lapps at, 65
Trondhjem (Tronyem) Fjord, scenery of, 113
Trondhjem, foundation of, by Olaf, 36; description of, 47; cathedral at, 48; environs of, 52; centre of traffic, 54; departure from, 55
Trout, abundance of, 17
Tvindefos, the, 146
Tyssestrangene, the, 141
Tyven, height of, 77

ULRICHSDAL (Oolricksdäl), 207
Ulvik Fjord, the, 145
Ulvik, situation of, 144
Upsala (Oopsåla), description of, 207; cathedral of, 208; university of, 209; castle of, 209
Utladal, valley of the, 150
Utne (Ootne), 133
Utvik, 121

VAAGEKELLE (Vögekellë), height of, 58
Vaags Fjord (Vögs), the, midnight sun at, 63
Vadheim, scenery at, 123; description of, 149
Vadsö, description of, 82
Valders district, the, description of, 157
Vangsmjösen (Vangsmyösen), 158
Vangsmjösen Lake, scenery of, 157
Vardö, description of, 81
Vardohus, the, 81
Vasendenfos, the, 139
Veblungsnæs, 110
Vener, Lake, area of, 214
Venersborg, description of, 215
Vermedalsfos, the, 108
Vest Fjord, the, 57
Vettersborg, castle at, 214
Vettifarm, 150
Vettifos, the, 150
Vik, or Wick (Veek), etymology of, 30
Vik, station at, 143
Viken, Lake, 214
Viking's ship, the, at Christiania, description of, 89
Vinje, 146
Vöringfos (Vëringfos), the, 141
Vossestrandselv, the, 146
Vossevangen, situation of, 146

WEDDINGS and wedding customs, 188
Worship, religious, 184
Wreta Church, 214

YULETIDE or Christmas, customs of, 33, 183

ILLUSTRATED BOOKS OF TRAVEL.

Australian Pictures:
DRAWN WITH PEN & PENCIL.

By **HOWARD WILLOUGHBY,**
OF "THE MELBOURNE ARGUS."

With a large Map and 107 Illustrations from Photographs and Sketches,
Engraved by E. WHYMPER and others.

Imperial 8vo. 8s. cloth boards, gilt edges; or 25s. in morocco, elegant.

COACHING SCENES.

ILLUSTRATED BOOKS OF TRAVEL.

NORWEGIAN PICTURES.

Drawn with Pen and Pencil.

With a glance at Sweden and the Gotha Canal.

By RICHARD LOVETT, M.A.

With a Map and One Hundred and Twenty-seven Illustrations, engraved by E. WHYMPER, R. TAYLOR, and others.

Imperial 8vo. 8s. cloth boards, gilt edges.

THE SVÆRHOLTKLUBBEN, OR BIRD ROCK.

ILLUSTRATED BOOKS OF TRAVEL.

OTTAWA.

CANADIAN PICTURES,

Drawn with Pen and Pencil.

By the MARQUIS OF LORNE, K.T.

With numerous Illustrations from Objects and Photographs in the possession of, and Sketches by, the MARQUIS OF LORNE, SIDNEY HALL, etc.

ENGRAVED BY EDWARD WHYMPER.

Imperial 8vo., elegantly bound in cloth, gilt edges, 8s.; morocco elegant, 25s.

ILLUSTRATED BOOKS OF TRAVEL.

SEA PICTURES.

Drawn with Pen and Pencil. By James Macaulay, M.A., M.D., Editor of the "Leisure Hour."

Imperial 8vo., handsomely bound, gilt edges, 8s.; *morocco elegant,* 25s.

CLOVELLY.

UNIFORM WITH THE ABOVE IN STYLE AND PRICE.

ENGLISH PICTURES.

DRAWN WITH PEN AND PENCIL.

By the Rev. S. MANNING, LL.D.,
and
Rev. S. G. GREEN, D.D.

With Coloured Frontispiece and Numerous Wood Engravings.

THE GRAMPIANS.

SCOTTISH PICTURES.
DRAWN WITH PEN AND PENCIL.
By SAMUEL G. GREEN, D.D.
Illustrated by Eminent Artists.
Imperial 8vo., handsomely bound, gilt edges, 8s; morocco elegant, 25s.

St. Ouen, Rouen.

Luther's House, Frankfurt.

FRENCH PICTURES,

DRAWN WITH PEN AND PENCIL.

By the Rev. Samuel G. Green, D.D. With upwards of 150 Fine Engravings.

Imperial 8vo., elegantly bound in cloth, gilt edges, 8s.; morocco, 25s.

PICTURES FROM THE GERMAN FATHERLAND,

Drawn with Pen and Pencil. By the Rev. Samuel G. Green, D.D. Profusely Illustrated with superior Engravings.

Bound in handsome cloth boards, full gilt, 8s.; morocco, 25s.

RUINS OF A SYNAGOGUE AT SHILOH.

THOSE HOLY FIELDS.
Palestine Illustrated by Pen and Pencil. By the Rev. Samuel Manning, LL.D.
With Numerous Fine Engravings.

COLUMNS OF TEMPLE AT LUXOR.

THE LAND OF THE PHARAOHS.
Egypt and Sinai Illustrated by Pen and Pencil. By the Rev. Samuel Manning, LL.D.
With Numerous Fine Engravings.
Imperial 8vo., elegantly bound in cloth, gilt edges, 8s. ; morocco, 25s.

ILLUSTRATED BOOKS OF TRAVEL.

SACRED TANK AND TEMPLE, MADURA.

Indian Pictures.
DRAWN WITH PEN AND PENCIL.
By the Rev. WILLIAM URWICK, M.A.
PROFUSELY ILLUSTRATED BY ENGLISH AND FOREIGN ARTISTS.
Imperial 8vo., handsomely bound, gilt edges, 8s.; *morocco, elegant,* 25s.

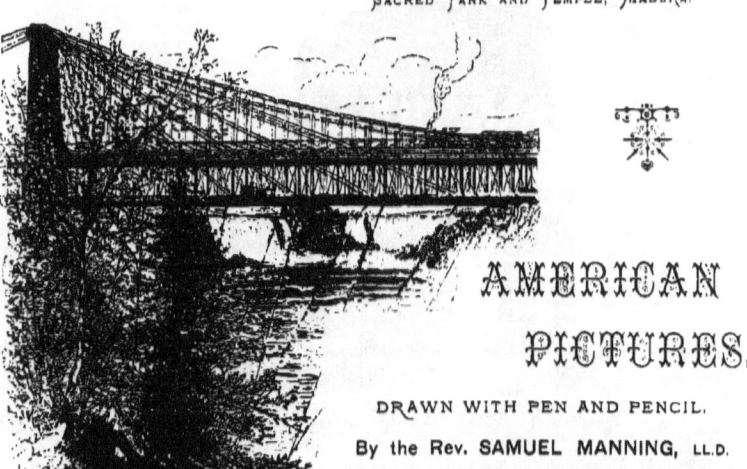

NIAGARA BRIDGE.

AMERICAN PICTURES.
DRAWN WITH PEN AND PENCIL.
By the Rev. SAMUEL MANNING, LL.D.
Profusely Illustrated in the best style of Wood Engraving by eminent English and Foreign Artists.
Imperial 8vo., elegantly bound in cloth, gilt edges, 8s.; *morocco,* 25s.

www.ingramcontent.com/pod-product-compliance
Lightning Source LLC
Chambersburg PA
CBHW020812230426
43666CB00007B/977